A BOOK OF CHINESE WHISPERS

KEN SMITH
A BOOK OF
CHINESE
WHISPERS

BLOODAXE BOOKS

821 SMI

47265

ISBN: 0 906427 93 2

First published 1987 by
Bloodaxe Books Ltd,
P.O. Box 1SN,
Newcastle upon Tyne NE99 1SN.

Bloodaxe Books Ltd acknowledges
the financial assistance of Northern Arts.

Typesetting by Bryan Williamson, Manchester.

Cover printing by
Tyneside Free Press Workshop Ltd, Newcastle upon Tyne.

Printed in Great Britain by
Robert Hartnoll (1985) Ltd, Bodmin, Cornwall.

Although my belief in the world returned to me, I have never since entirely freed myself of the impression that this life is a segment of existence enacted in a three-dimensional boxlike universe especially set up for it . . .

It is important and salutary to speak also of incomprehensible things.

– Carl Gustav Jung: *Memories, Dreams, Reflections*

Acknowledgements

Some of these pieces originally appeared in magazines and chapbooks, and to the editors and publishers of these thanks are due: **Casual Labour** appeared in *Tangent*; **Not quite Buster Keaton** in *Poetry Review*; **Ektachrome** in *Not Poetry*; and **One of our objects is missing** in *South West Review*, pseudonymously under Jack Streaky.

The atmospheric railway up to and including *The makings* was published in two editions of *Frontwards in a backwards movie* (1974, 1977) by Arc & Throstle Press. *The wild turkey* was published as a broadside from Cat's Pajamas Press (Illinois) in 1975, and **Island called Henry the Navigator** as a chapbook also from Cat's Pajamas (1976). The remainder of **The atmospheric railway** formed a pamphlet brought out by X Press in 1980, *The joined-up writing*, in an edition that was for reasons best known to its editor destroyed soon thereafter. *The night boat* was anthologised in *Poetry of the Committed Individual*, published by *Stand*, Penguin Books and Victor Gollancz.

The wild rose was published as a chapbook in 1973 by Stinktree Press (Memphis). **Anus Mundi** was published by Four Zoas (Massachusetts) in 1976.

From **Invisible thread**, *The blinding* appeared in *Ironwood*, and with *And other tales* in *Ambit*. *Dreaming of horses, Ripon revisited, Russians invented the neutron bomb, The discovery of secret theatre*, and *Cogito at the British Museum* appeared in *London Magazine*; *The poetry reading* in *Iron*; *Problems of a northern boyhood* in *Oxford Poetry Society Broadsheet*; and *Misericorde, Magic liquid, The left slipper* and *At the Mirabelle* in *Stride*.

The photographs are by Irene Reddish (pages 11, 53, 95 & 127), Tom Nickerson (47 & 115) and Kate Mellor (107).

Contents

SWISS WARBLER BIRD CALL

Directions for use: Soak in water until thoroughly saturated. Place on tongue with membrane nearest the teeth and finished side of leather upwards. Hiss gently at first, increasing the hiss for a louder sound. The tongue and lips can be used to make various birdlike imitations.

Distributed by Mechanical Servants, Inc. Chicago, Illinois 60640

Made in Japan

CAUTION

Keep this away from small children who may swallow it.

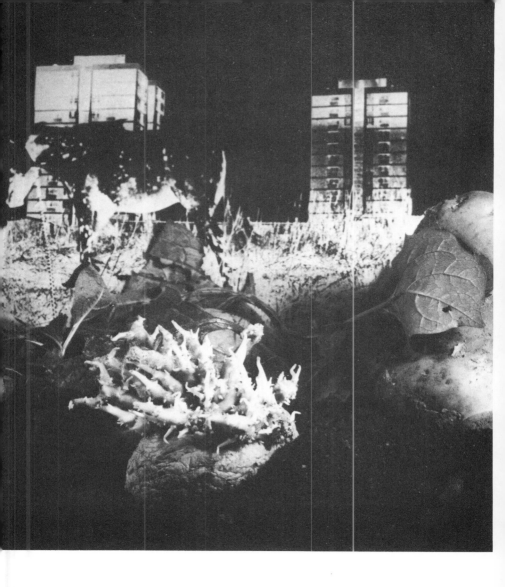

Casual labour

Ancient history

Before the potato, men scratched the earth with sticks or crouched under rocks waiting for the weather to improve. But the introduction of the potato changed history when Lord Rally came over the ocean. Since then, thousands of years ago, our people have picked potatoes on the estates of Lord Clifton. We have known nothing else, nor wish to, for we are pickers first and last. Five days a week, all year around, for a full five shillings, there are potatoes to pick from sea to shining sea.

The preface

In an eight hour day a good picker can fill 100 paper sacks with potatoes, each sack containing 56 lbs. I prefer to work with two baskets, myself. It saves walking, and two good baskets fill a sack. I've found the quickest method is to work two rows together, standing legs apart between them, filling each basket on either side of my feet. I pick from the furthest inwards, and use the gloves to protect my hands and give myself a bigger grasp. If by chance I pick stones instead of potatoes I chuck them in too. My one rule is: *if I pick it up it's a potato.* As I work I search for the golden potato, for it is said that through these fields Lord Clifton has distributed so many golden potatoes that entitle the finders to special privileges. But for myself, I am beginning to doubt the existence of golden potatoes. I am beginning to suspect a trick.

Genesis

First darkness, then light. It rained for forty nights and days, but the lads went on picking just the same. Lord Rally built a little boat to sail upon the flood, and came to the shores of Potato Mother's Land. Lord Rally sent out a dove, the dove came back with a tuber in its mouth, and from the tuber sprang the potato plant. Lord Rally rolled up some of its leaves, and from this came tobacco. He picked off some of the fruits and ate them. From this came the tomato. Last he came to the roots, and found there the potatoes, which he boiled and ate. Then Lord Rally had a vision, or – as some call it – a mystical experience, or as he says in *Lord Rally's Logbook*, he experienced 'a state of non-ordinary reality. Terrific!' Lord Rally returned to Yetterton in Devon to find

the flood had gone and there he planted, in these very fields we pick
my brothers, the original potato plant from whose issue this our harvest
springs. That's how we got the potato, children. And that's why, every
year in spring on the anniversary of Lord Rally's return, Lord Clifton
walks to the centre of his estates and there releases a white dove.

Potato olympics

Early morning hangover handicap. Missing the bus and trying to catch
up. Three-legged picking. Putt the basket. Tossing the King Edward.
Fighting thistles. Hurling spuds about. Stopping others work. Sore
Knee Shuffle, 300 metres. Work till you drop. Filling someone else's
bag by mistake. Picking blind. Staggering home. Forgetting how many
bags you've picked. Sitting in the trailer. Waiting for the foreman.
Spending it as quickly as you can.

The commentary

Well Roger this is an interesting field we have here and we have seen
some very fine picking till now but as to who will come out with most
bags this week well it is piece-work and just about anything could happen
but Roger if you ask me Stagehand has the showing. He's pretty well
placed there on the outside by the hedge, the slope is with him, he's
sheltered from the drizzle, and there's the double planting of the head-
land in his favour. As you know he's been pacing himself well the last
couple of weeks, he's at the top of his form and he has the will to come
out ahead. Mind you Roger if you'd asked me a couple of days ago I
would have tipped Dancer. He's big that lad and very strong and those
long arms of his give him a tremendous reach, and he does have the
advantage of years of ballet training that equip him very well now for
the potato picking. As he himself said the other day *there's nae tae mony
vacancies fra mael dauncers in Glasgae*. But he's been slowing down, and
I suspect the amount of beer he's been putting away in Sidmouth. Well
Roger they're off and as they go into the curve it's Stagehand then
Dancer. Dancer's morale seems to be slipping already as he pauses to
spit and curse the paper sack that's just split on him. Then it's Zen
Buddhist, picking very well today, followed by Androgyny and the Mac-
robiotic Twins. Then Poet. Then Irishman. Then comes Actor, who'll

14

probably knock off at lunch to go collect his social security again, then comes the pack hanging about by the trailer, and lastly off to a late start The Bloke With The Black Dog. It's still Stagehand's field, but there's a long day ahead of us and anything could happen yet. The unknown, The Bloke With The Black Dog, picks like a maniac at times. Just between the two of us Roger he's a very dirty picker and only takes the big ones but there we are Nigel, filling sacks is the name of the game.

Some inventions that failed

As I worked I considered methods of simplifying the potato picking. I proposed planting seed in baskets so that collecting the crop later in the year became a matter of picking up the baskets and shaking out the soil. Then, in the laboratory of my skull, I developed potatoes with a thin metal strip at one end, so all the pickers had to do was walk along the field with powerful magnets. All this of course done without the knowledge of Lord Clifton or the foreman or the tractor driver, who though he wears earmuffs isn't blind. My mate, Duncan, wondered might it not be possible to develop a potato with a small pocket under its jacket like the air space in an egg. Within the space the potato would accumulate hydrogen to lift itself out of the ground when ripe, hovering there waiting to be basketed. We considered briefly a feasibility study during a smoke break, hired a market research team and computer time and canvassed investment in the project before stooping to pick another umpteen sacks. At lunch, eating marrow jam sandwiches in the trailer, I proposed to the Great Potato Mother Convention in Minneapolis a scheme for the self-picking potato, the SPP. The SPP grew little arms and legs. When ready, all Lord Clifton need do would be to walk through the fields playing Rose of Tralee on a little pipe, and all the potatoes would climb out of the ground and into the paper sacks, shaking themselves clean as they did so. And might they not peel themselves too? Aye, they might, Duncan affirmed, his mouth full of sandwich, his thermos gripped between his wellies. And where would we be, tell me that? Laid off again. Painting railway stations. Shuttering on the motorway if there's any motorway left to shutter. On the Lump, or selling encylopaedias. Or down the dole office answering daft questions like who shot the turkey and how many bishops in Spain?

The middle ages

In this period everyone worked his own patch. They ate sandwiches even on Sundays. And if they spoke at all spoke in grunts and had their heads chopped off for even that: 'nowt but mice, lice and bad advice'. It was like South Africa for three million years. The potatoes were very small, and you heard the continual music of the first three bars of the Harry Lime Theme, over and over. Fortunately things improved. The Ice Age, the Iron Age, the Romans, the Beaker People came and went in swift succession, followed by the signing of the Magna Carta, that put an end to tyrannies so absolute we are forbidden even now to mention them.

The scene that day

The scene that day was of a sloping field in intermittent sunlight. A dozen or so pickers picked the potatoes up and down the slope, each his own patch. Later a woman came with a boy, finding it difficult to establish her own space. The trailer was moved at midday closer to the pickers. The foreman drove up in his landrover a couple of times, consulted with the tractor driver, went away again. He did his business, yet seemed permanently abstracted, as if he lived within his own body and profession by accident, his life being somewhere else perhaps. Likewise the tractor driver, keeping a general though not lofty distance from the pickers, with whom he occasionally conversed. Otherwise he lived in his glass-cabbed tractor, moving up and down the field, his earmuffs shutting out the sound he made. From time to time, we noticed, he placed a little white pill from a phial on his tongue, and took a swig from his water bottle. Asked, he spoke of them as *his pills*, and smiled vaguely from somewhere in the interior of himself.

The coming of the Potato Mother

Potato Mother came, and blessed the barren fields. And the Lord Clifton went in unto the Potato Mother back at the big house. Potato Mother conceived and brought forth the primal potato, and there was wide rejoicing. Men gathered in groves of the forest to sing her praises. No more need they plant stones and weep over thistles. Thus ended centuries

16

when potatoes had to be carved from pine cones and boiled for years before they became succulent. Oh Potato Mother, Our Soft Lady Willendorf, Little Sister of the First Water, may we lie in thy fields forever, thou who hast given us the potato, from which we make boots, and clothes, and books, and tractors, and which we eat and dry for fuel. Without thee Potato Mother would we not be crouching under rocks to this day, eating snails?

The picker's prayer

Potato Mother, may thy potatoes be fat and plentiful with weeds and stones few and may they leap into my baskets, yea may they leap into my sacks, that my weariness at day's end be rewarded amply, amen.

The picker's heaven

No more potatoes, Sunday forever, no rain, no mucky boots, cracked nails, dust in my eyes, stones in my shoe. But the pay envelopes still come, it's best piece-work, it's 1976, and there's a pub at the corner of the field selling cider at 1958 prices. So here I am in the public, waiting to be reborn to spend the next few million lifetimes as a Colorado beetle. *Zix mower points yer scrumpie yer lanlord, yer be afercrown, Gorbless yer.*

The potato wars

We are potatory says Davie. And this, says he of his 11th pint of hard cider, is our potation. From his pocket he takes a potato. This is our Roundhead potato. The Royalists, the King Edwards, have been disallowed under Common Market rules. He puts the potato beside his drink, and takes from his other pocket another potato. Now this, this is your smoothie, your bureaucrat potato, your Common Market spud. Oh the wars were terrible while they lasted. Some were for putting razor blades in the soup and going over with spikes and broken bottles to the next field to fight it out. But Lord Clifton in his merciful temperance and justice persuaded us against it. Instead, suggested he, why not pack the potatoes full of high explosive and old chain, roll them

17

down the enemy's rabbit holes, and blow them out of their beds? So
we did, and disabled their tractors and kicked hell out of their baskets.
But now the wars are over, and we're not sorry, even though we lost.

From the picker songbook

Potatoes out of Idaho,
Potatoes out of France,
Grow big and fat and plentiful
And in my basket dance.

Two by two, two by two,
Potatoes in their jackets,
Fill the baskets,
Fill the bags,
Fill up my paypackets.

Lord Rally, Lord Rally,
went riding one day,
And met an old picker
Along the highway.

His clothes were in tatters,
His boots were in bits,
For with stooping and picking
He'd picked through his wits.

Old picker, old picker
Says Rally to him,
Your rows be all pickered,
Your sacks be all in.

Lord Rally, Lord Rally,
The picker he said,
I may be picked over
But they'll pick off your head.

And that was what happened –
Lord Rally got chopped.
So don't count your potatoes
Before they're all cropped.

And that is my moral,
The theme of my song,
As I pick the potatoes
The green fields among.

The triumph of Lord Rally

Oh ar er lived down yer a bit. Roit bugger ee as put eez coat in road
fer Queen an ey do zay ee ad eez wicked way of er an er a virgin all er
dayz. Zounz mazed er. Ztill talk about ee round yer. Zome zay az Drake
carn't ztomach ee, bit of a fancy bloke Oi reckon, carn't old ez zoider.
But ee were roit good elmsman, landed genry or nor, bettern Drake.
Drake a good steerzman, oh ar, an engineer, built Plymouth Leat up
Dartmoor, Oi zeen er. Go for miles Jahn. Courz Rally were squoir yer,
eerz yer taterz whor ee bror from New World. Er were Red Indian
crorp, grew in little heaps, fore Rally ad er. 'Ar,' zayz ee when eez in
Armericer an ee zeez a few of ey, 'Troy a few back yer in Collerton
Rally.' An ee shipz ome a ton er two. Ey growz or right, ey bloddy growz
Jahn. But eze yer no good, ey too zmall ey, geddyorf. Tiz drought tiz.
Tiz drought. An now eyz pickin ey erz bloddy rainin pigz bladderz. An
tiz Common Market. Tizn juss drought forcin prizez up, tiz ey boggerz
drinkin tea in bloddy Bruzzelz, bureaucratz, bloddy Bruzzelz sproutz
more loike. Zcrumpie dizappearin. Now erz zame proiz as beer, zpend
a bloddy fortune in yer uz doz eh Jahn? Could have a good laugh fer a
tanner onze, night out on afercrown, counzil houzez zix fer a shillin an
even little lambs ad underpantz on. Ere. Funny lot that thar. Cazul
labour. Uzul crew er layaboutz, labour egzchange an zochial zecurity
zcruffz, ippiez an a. When Oi were a lad er were moztly kidz an women,
ad a week off zchool fer er, potato pickin an larkin about. Blokez squeezin
wormz an at Jahn, women az ad takee in a bushez, in em dayz. Now
itz yer airy ippiez an eez yer from Zidmouth zmokin er funny zigarettez.

A new phase: we meet the running dogs and fascist lackeys of capitalism and imperialism. The east wind no longer prevails and the black gang seizes the means of production.

First drive off the smallholders, promising new land in the middle of the Atlantic. Our banks foreclose on their mortgages. Bulldozers and rentacops knock down hedges and villages, and we plant the land with potatoes from horizon to horizon. A man may walk from dawn to dusk seeing nothing but potatoes yet not leave one field of our domains. The people live in pickers' barracks and work for nothing save a little meat, cheap beer, and as many potatoes as they can steal. We export the surplus, underselling everyone else and crippling the economies of emergent nations, bringing on world famine which we cure by exchanging potatoes for complete economic and political control. Then we take over the world, live lives of responsible and spartan luxury, organise everything down to the last teaspoon, and grow potatoes on every available inch. As for this Marx fellow, he gets to pick a hundred sacks a day, and peel them too, for the rest of his rotten life.

The totalitarian potato

Anyone who isn't a potato picker, a chargehand, tractor driver or foreman is scum, and will be sent to pick in the Antarctic. Anyone who doesn't volunteer for double shifts will be poked in both eyes. Anyone who doesn't sing aloud all 27 verses of *Potato Pickers of Collaton Raleigh Rejoice in the New Five Year Plan and Unite to Defeat the Enemy* all day as he works will have his bags tipped out and start again. Anyone who doesn't pick seven days a week all hours and weathers will be sent to live underground. I, the Little Father of the Potato Nation, have spoken. *Edict One:* No stones, no muck, and no rotten spuds. *Edict Two:* the insidious religion of the Potato Mother banned. *Edict Three:* pickers to commence growing shorter, starting now, developing large flat feet, long arms and large hands with at least ten fingers on each hand. *Edict Four:* secret. *Edict Five:* use of language spoken or written hereby reserved solely for government use; pickers read this and the next three edicts, then nothing else: no one teach it, write it, speak or sing it without licence from the nearest post office. *Edict Six:* suspension of postal services; all post offices to be demolished immediately; anyone who can still read and write better forget it or else, this is punk potato power speaking; we want nothing but grunts and snarls from you lot – snaps and whimpers, male chauvinist guffaws, groans, pleas for mercy, snoring, that's O.K. Anything else is treason, mutiny, sabotage, piracy, interference with interstate commerce, rebellion, and makes you go blind. *Edict Seven:* all the women come and live in the big house with us. *Edict Eight:* watch it that's all.

The peasant revolt

Funny, the foreman says. It happens every year. They pick for a month and then walk off. Nick's asleep under the tractor. It's raining again. Charley tips out his half-filled sack and rips it up. He kicks over more sacks. *They bags cost nine pence each*, the foreman says, *and we pay you ten pence per bag to fill 'em.* Charley begins kicking baskets. *Profiteering mother-robbing sweated labour slave-driving black hearted sons of fatherless bitches.* The Jesus Freaks move to cut him off, but the revolt spreads down the rows: one by one the pickers look up to see Mick wearing the tractor driver's earmuffs, and Nick and Charley tipping everyone's bags unless they'll pack up and go down the pub. The whole field walks off and stays off all day while the foreman sits in the landrover cursing Lord Clifton's potatoes. Who would have thought the final death agonies of capitalism would turn out to be so few and simple?

Potatoism

Now we have the Revolution. Terrific. The land, the potatoes, the baskets, bags, tractors, machinery, barns, landrovers, telephones, all belong to the people. The women come back. Sometimes we go north along the shores of the big water, the picking's good there, once I saw a blue heron that had stood for an hour without moving rise in the great smokey wingspread of himself and fly all ease and grace across the estuary. Oh we like working now it's the Revolution. This year we're once more hoping for yet another bumper harvest yet again. Next year we will greet a delegation of carrot pickers from the New Surbiton Collectives. Everything's fine now: schools, hospitals, main drainage and TV. There's minimum hours and old-age pensions, the state has withered away and it's the end of history. We don't mind the extra effort, not when it's for the Revolution. Some days a pheasant breaks from

21

from cover close by and goes whirring and rust across the tops, men trying to down him for dinner, it's like the planet paused in its spin, the world *there* again, childhood and summer, all history a babble through the mind and we speak again, love, in no one else's language.

A picker's humble question

What was it St Francis preached to the birds about?

The end of all history

That all came out jumbled in all the different heads, Napoleon v. Attila the Hun, Marie Antoinette in bed with Nostradamus, the Romans agreeing at last to sign the human rights charter at Runnymede and grant majority rule within two years. And so forth. Words words words, example: *potato* from Spanish *patata* from Carib Taino *batata*, meaning unknown; example *avocado* from Spanish *aquacate* from Nahuatl *ahuacatl*, meaning testicle. Oh ar Oi loiks er bit er specerlatin moiself Oi do, the odd ounze come in roit andy when erz tattyin to do. But yet I think there must be someone else beside me on this endless field, or am I all alone, working in the rain, assuring myself my boots don't leak, asking who makes these gloves, and these shiny metal buttons stamped ARMY? Someone must weave these blue shirts, the colour of the sky beyond these clouds, someone must have invented this language I speak to myself in. Very interesting. But with all these spuds to pick in the piddling rain I've no more time to think about it. I've these bags to fill before dark, and potatoes don't pick themselves.

Atmospheric Railway

In Paris, in the Twenties, with Bell. Yours ever.

It's a trick: cut out photographs of people and stick them side by side, close the shutter. You get people together who couldn't stand each other and may never have met. Still if Widsith can bring together the lovers divided and delivered centuries apart, we should be free to make fabulous marriages. So much for collage, I said. And so much for my Wanderjahren, I've already pawned my notebooks of le petomane inscribed to me and my picture of the lost president and my permit to visit freely. Down on the quay two little girls were singing

> *We have to write to Robert Bly*
> *About the gardens at Versailles.*

I move on, under the bulges of the cops, past the drunks and ghosts. Think of Tennyson, who died with 'his hand on his Shakespeare'. It needs retouching. And even now I don't know what to do about childhood, which seems to have gone off with its spotted handkerchief and pole across its shoulder.

Votive

Much of me is gregarious. I like talk, though it accomplishes little, because I love language, which makes the world real to me. Those who know me know me only through speaking, they do not know that I do not prefer conversations. That much of me that does not know cannot be known easily. This is the man who turns towards silence.

But I am solitary so as to go to the country of solitude. When I come back to the country of the blind I want to speak about silence and what I have heard there. It is difficult dealing with things the blind think they see. It is like speaking of the ocean to people who have lived all their lives in the interior: they think of the sea only as water. Similarly it is hard to describe horses to those who have never experienced them. I try to provide their smells and the sounds of their bodies heaving a plough and the way they sleep standing in the darkness. I try to suggest them through the flick of their manes and the way they roll in the paddock and the brown touch of their sweats at harvest. No one can remember horses. Because of this I become sociable. I want to hear how it is in this strange place.

25

The begging woman

And old woman came to my house, asking to sleep on the porch. It was autumn, a clear night with the moon shining, peachblow on porcelain. I was embarrassed but could not refuse. Clearly the woman was destitute, a vagrant in place after place, begging. I should have invited her into the house. I thought of her smell: sweat, urine, the fetor of long worn clothing, weariness. Talking to her I recognised her accent as my own: a woman from my own country. *Yes, but I have been here longer than you* she replied. I thought for something to give her and brought from the house coins I had saved from the country we both came from. I had kept them for sentiment, they were useless here. I held them out to her. She turned away: that was old money, no longer in use there, valueless in either kingdom.

Man, wife: American Gothic

The river digs itself out through its own deposit. The years spent working into bedrock, stones flailing stones, are not compensated; the generations of chalk, the flash-flood that left a thin razor of slate, they are cut through at random. The shale falls in from each bank, the clays are broken and carried off, there are shallows and deeper places, the bottom clogs again. All that happens happens in season: the stream falls and rises, breaks corners, cuts new channels, finds a longer way.

Over the low hills they come and go raising their pennants. In time each mound flutters a white flag. They address each other: *I have forgiven you this, I forgive you such and such.* It is the same as not forgiving. They are aware of the sea one way where the silts fan out offshore. And sometimes they speak of the river's beginning in the rain and the moor's leakage – a thin clear energy, a single finger of water.

Dinger's Farm

Grass struggles between the stones, the stones shatter under the sun. It is a shingle where there is no sea; thistles, a few shrubs, aspens shivering in the brilliant waste.

I have this house, the barn with nothing in it, a bit of garden for vegetables. Last year she grew sunflowers, nothing but sunflowers. My people were from Holland, I speak no Dutch and I don't know what their name was before it was Dinger. I had two sons, gone now, don't know where. And a daughter. She married and went off, had a postcard from her one time, Tiffin, Ohio. Don't know if she's still there. I farmed in Idaho, then Indiana. Then I come here. Grew the best corn in the county, sweeter than milk. Won prizes, red ribbons, yellow ribbons. Never used fertiliser, just lime. This was a good place. Strippers came by, said I had coal in there and wanted it. I said no. But she got sick, the hospital wouldn't take payments. Had to have money before they'd operate. It was my wife or my farm so I sent to the strippers and they took it all out and here I am with a house and a barn and a crazy woman. I was a good farmer.

The Island

I remember a weed-stain on water, the fish that left only the ripple of its track. That distant Sargasso builds to mountains, the rock goes down into its pressures, there are fields, the signs of men long sunk into the lands they worked. It is an odour I catch sometimes, – hyacinth, the pines stirred by a light rain at evening –, it vanishes as it is noticed, like the fish. Long beads of traffic follow the hill, the sheep peer down into the settlements, the grey towns that have broken their limits.

The island has fallen from my hands like a dropped plate into the bits it makes. It is a light, the exact shape of childhood.

The Scythians

Herodotus tells how they cut off the heads of their enemies. The women fought beside the men; before she could marry a girl must kill an enemy in battle.

They lie under the mounds they built, the bones as if ready to rise to mount their horses and vanish. They are held down by the iron plates they wore in combat. They are here with their gold and the beaten metal shapes of strange animals that will appear centuries later on the shields of Europe's factions, with their slaves strangled beside them, their tools and weapons, bowls of food and hemp seed for the journeys. The plain wind blows through them, the sky holds them down and the loess supports them. For all their fierceness they were gracious to their victims. Before burial they patiently sewed back the scalps they had taken, that even their enemies might not be without dignity in the other world.

Lake Harvey

Worked out horses were dropped in on ropes, pulled up a fortnight later full of eels. The lake is so deep there are said to be glaciers at the bottom. In the nineteenth century a carriage with horses and passengers fell into it. They froze down there. Divers have seen them, the travellers with their faces and gestures of horror, their conversations forever interrupted.

There are those who struggle so hard to live they become denials, shutting themselves from the life they desire.

In Aprile

I arrive at airports after the last plane has gone. Short of money, I try to sleep on the benches, the officials throw me out. They say *people who cannot afford hotels cannot afford airplanes*. I watch the limousines leaving like long hearses for the Hotel Kafka. The passengers count their travellers' cheques, rehearsing their names for the desk clerk. I walk around in the night. There are fuel trucks and small tractors and everywhere men who have become the servants of the machines. Wherever I am, I am in someone's way, but there is nowhere to go.

I ask for the time of the next plane, the first plane in the morning, any plane, going anywhere. There are no more planes. The airport is closed. Not closed for the night, closed down. I have a ticket, but there is nowhere to go.

At last I find a place to sleep. It is always difficult, sleeping in clothes, they tighten in the crutch and under the arms and as sleep comes there

28

is always an itch somewhere that must be seen to. Lying on my side the coins in my pocket dig into my thigh. As I fall asleep I decide to get rid of them, to have no money, for it is when I have nothing I discover my luck. Hungry, I enter a restaurant where I order a meal in perfect Cantonese, even remembering the words for the Chinese tea that is secret whisky. Finally I order a tray of fortune cookies. In each one I find the same message: *get out, get out*. I struggle towards waking, where I shall find myself, hungry and irritable, with the money still in my pocket.

On the Spanish River

Amongst the people of the delta there is a culture of darkness many centuries old. Around it circle the rhythms of the year's work, their ceremonies, and all their relationships with each other. Darkness is cured in three ways:

Salting. The darkness is collected and heaped in the courtyard. The people use a rock salt ground to powder mixed with urine and pork fat. They rub the mix in with their fingers very slowly over one week of the new moon. As the work goes on the dark is teased out into strands that are bound into a thick rope for storing. Everyone participates in the work equally. Darkness treated in this way ensures anonymity and can be woven to make a cloak of invisibility. It is used especially in wrapping the dead for burial.

Smoking. The darkness is cut into lengths and hung from a pole in the central hut. The old men and the younger men selected for the work sit around the strips in a circle. They smoke a mixture of dried herbs and pounded roots, passing the pipes to each other, always to the left. They must inhale deeply, and they must breathe out very slowly over the strips. It is a long process during which no man may speak to his neighbours until he receives his name from the smoke. When all have been named the curing is done, each man speaks his name in turn. The lengths of darkness have turned to a deep shining black. They are rolled into bundles for storing and put away for as long as possible. The longer the better.

Drying. In summer the darkness is pegged down on flat ground. The women and girls dance on it to paddle it to a thin sheet, dancing for three days to instruments played by the men. On the third day the cantor comes and sings over the darkness: *dark, we have abandoned you.* But for the cantor everyone leaves the village, swearing aloud they will never return. A light rain falls, and then for three days the darkness lies in the sun while the cantor watches it; he must neither close his eyes nor turn them away. After three days he too leaves the village and calls out to the people hiding in the forest. They return. The darkness has dried to a sheer white. Properly cured in this way, it will last forever.

The magician

He kept a cupboard where he sat saying aloud with Vespasian, dying, *alas, I think I am becoming a god.* In the cupboard were jars labelled in alphabetical order and in them all the myths hardening into tropes, in this one a feather of the swan she was when he first took her, in that the small pillar of salt she had become when he turned back for her, seeing her as she really was. He would inspect the jars, dusting like a housewife, holding them to the light that came out of them, blue, yellow, green, like a chemist's shop full of liquids. His jars were Procrustean, they contained mementos: the score of the Sirens' song, the eye of the Cyclops, the two eyes of Oedipus, the three faces of Janus and the watchings of all the gods. He preserved a bottle of the burned dust of Troy, all its speech become grey and featureless, the ashes of a book of obscene drawings of Penelope. Here was the snakey head of Medusa reduced to abstraction with no other world to guard, and Charon's ferry pass, and the looking glass that turned the watchers to stones, and the double axe that was the key to the labyrinth that was no mystery but merely the winding house of the axe and the power at the maze's end to reduced everything to nothing.

He opens a jar, he examines the hemlock seeds gathered by Socrates' grateful student who scooped up whatever he could market. He opens another, it contains the blood of the young man innocently slain that will grow into a flower in any place but a jar. He lifts the lid of a third and listens to the singing head of Orpheus, its melody accompanied by the sounds of the rushing stream. This is as far as he goes. He writes on the paper *shah mat, the king is dead.* And picks up his hat, his gloves, his cane.

Anselm at the Neverness Motel

Since it's part of the rent I switch on the TV but forget to watch it. The strange blue faces swim in from the other side of town. I can go out and spend money or stay here and spend money, listening to the lovers in the corridor walking so their footsteps leave no echoes. Reading the magazines I see tidy fields and girls, they have breasts like daffodils, they invite me to vacations I don't need with poolside bars and the rooms cleansed by invisible hands. And it can be mine on credit cards and easy payments, memories I will store against winter, sinning in crisp white sheets, a flower crushed in the Gideon and her bra in my briefcase. Ah, the long evenings of dancing and drinks on the terrace, I could be famous and mysterious, leaving big tips and hinting assignments and numerous bank accounts and fishing in Canada and saying *at the Berghof.* And here is the picture of the smile I will use and here's who I'll be and here is the man you all know by the sign you all know.

Ultima Thule

As the saying is, *in a crisis put out a colony.* Taxes were raised, the boats built and rigged. Many had work then until the boats left, full of riffraff, port rats and bad apples, nudging into the coastal sea. Sails cracked under the wind, the sea opening before and closing behind. They were like so many loaves of bread on the ocean.

Storms, mists, hidden reefs carried off some. Too much wind or too little, the tale is familiar. Beyond the eastern sea we sailed on the shoulders of the trade winds, long out of sight of land, lost in the wastes. Men spoke of their homes, of women they knew, staring out into the wind as if they might see them in the shapes of familiar headlands or the formations of clouds. Murder and mutiny took some, scores were settled, salt and cold drove men mad. We sailed in a great circle passing, in the south, islands of weeds, in the north islands of drifting ice. We could set foot on neither. There was no land other than the lands we knew, green and rearing before the prows of ships, beaches of white distant bone, the hills a darker blue than the sky. Nor, when we came full circle under the stars' pointers, could we find our home, crossing over and over the exact place it should have been and seeing only the waters' heaving, green weeds, a bit of carved wood, a chairpost, and a raft to which was lashed a dead man and a broken amphora where a few gold coins still remained. They were unfamiliar, cut with a script none of us recognised and the head of a king no one knew. We still keep them, though they serve no purpose here where no one comes. We live in this rocky place with what we have saved, with our goats and a few stunted bushes, where the stones make the wind cry with its uselessness.

My country

is always of the high grass. Higher, nearer the sun, the summer grass parches and suddenly blazes. As the slopes level out the bracken takes over, and beyond on the flat moors only the heather wins behind dry stone walls put up by the monks centuries gone. A pheasant, a moorhen, the wind; there are few sounds. The Swale turns through its valley, stones glint in its bed, the trout vanishes: the river of loneliness, clear as the first water. At night on the hills the farmers turn up their lamps, the villages glitter like stars through their Viking names: Askrigg, Marske, Keld. The valley places are Saxon. The map has few names. It is a country of gutturals and thin reaping, living in it there is little to say.

To return, to go there, accomplishes nothing. I find the labourers bent in their silence, brooding. I do not know what they want. On Sundays their voices flow through the chapels and the preachers name them the sins, one by one. For all their singing they cannot get into heaven, the way is blocked by the slaughtered: blood eagles, leathery Benedictines, the Methodists' tight mouths, the farmers cursed by their chickens. They praise God, and over their heads the prayers clatter against each other.

A memorable fancy

It occurred to me that time is a huge spring approaching its recoil. One day we may find ourselves drinking a coffee or buttoning a shirt. There will be a slight pause and we will begin unbuttoning a shirt and undrinking the coffee. Everything we have done we will do one more time in reverse order, and so backwards as history rolls itself up. Everything

32

will be repeated: St Francis would preach to the birds again until the idea leaves him and he becomes just another restless young man, we would watch the candles growing from their pools of wax, the egg would lay itself and the clocks run backwards. We would refight all the wars, for nothing, battling back through Europe till Hitler disappears into some obscure lodging house in the years of confusion that last until the war begins again and again ceases and there are only rumours of war and the world we know loses itself in its origins. The planes would give place to old models and pioneering experiments until the idea of flying becomes merely a dream, the birdman falling from the Eiffel Tower, Cyrano proposing a journey to the moon in a basket pulled by swans, Leonardo losing the sketch he made for a flying machine until he is only a boy frowning vaguely at a heron. The radio would reach 1930, 1926, we would begin calling it the wireless with its reports on Russia and the big strike till a squeaky voice is saying *hello hello is anyone there* and the telephone rings for the last time with no one answering till it is dismantled and the voices are silent.

Recently, sawing logs, thinking of an old continent weary of battering itself, I thought of it as a spent bullet. Seconds later the saw cried through metal and I found just such a bullet buried in the tree. And later, driving to no place and talking of nothing, Claude said *we are going frontwards in a backwards movie.*

Nick's story

We went to sleep. The children dreamed they were in a strange house. They went into a closet and saw that all the clothes were old-fashioned, gowns and capes from another century with ribbons that had not yet faded. Also in there were things you see in museums: penny farthings, hoops and mangles and mincers, a writing desk that opened out into a sort of boat in case of shipwreck. Then the children came out of the closet, out of the house and down the road. A woman came from her cottage, calling them in to supper. *But you're not our mother* they said, though they went in anyway. After supper the woman told them to go to bed. Again they said they did not live here, they were not her children. *Yes* said the woman *I am your mother*. And she insisted it was time for bed. So they went to bed and slept. They dreamed, and in the dream they returned to the strange house that was deserted with all its furniture and clothing, and they went out again through the closet and into the garden with its empty swing and its flowers and bushes gone wild and fruit trees turned bitter. There their own mother called them in to supper. And they went in and found that their mother was the woman who had called them before.

Maison des illusions

The taxi leaves, the bell rings, the maid welcomes the new arrivals: the butcher, the baker, the candlestick maker. Down the corridor the curtains blow in the incoming breeze. The guests name their desires and are shown to their rooms where they drop the latch. They think of the words they will use when they meet later in the Tivoli Bar. Men come here bringing gifts – little statues of themselves, trinkets, promises cast in the Seine. The water slowly demolishes them. They become pitted, a treasury of wants. In the rooms sit the girls, surrounded by their objects. The legislators come and go: the knight, the bishop, their faces drawn to the bone. Here is the President Perdu who deals only with a little dark girl from the south and speaks to her in Italian, which is not her language, about his plans for the new forum. He promises to marry her, that she will sit at his side in the grand box in the football stadium, they will go to America, she will have a wallet full of credit cards. He pays for her time in the old imperial currency but the madame receives a state cheque on the first of the month. Night by night the great ghosts arrive leaving behind them their silver coins and their bad poems, they write obscenities on the toilet walls and from their beds they offer up the iron prayers of the crusaders. The cleaning woman gathers up their footprints. She pastes them in a scrapbook and dreams of the day she will publish them, a story for her grandchildren, a little blackmail perhaps. For her it is a question of logistics, she is like the general remembering his errors of judgement. Whether he recolours the maps of Europe or she mops the floor it is all a question of moving wisely across spaces.

Boudicca

To the north of us is a people living on islands of weed. For them the world is a circle of water, hell on one shore, heaven on the other. Unlike us they do not expect the ground to sustain them, even in death. To the east there is nothing but water, with land beyond about which we know nothing. It is said men walk on their hands there, that they sleep in the day and work through the nights and that whoever would trade with them must meet them at twilight. West of us lie the flatlands where people live as we do, and far beyond them the mountains and the sea again. The mountain people sleep with goats and sheep, they are half goat themselves. They believe god is a great eye wandering in mists, that his touch is like wet fern and his anger a ram's horn. There is nothing to fear from any of them. Only from the south danger comes, where the gods are fiercely shaped stones and the people live in two worlds, one of incense and chanting, the other of knives and economics. While they blind you with one they cut you down with the other. They want lead, silver, tin, wheat. What they want is not singing.

The dead give up nothing without struggle. They must be spoken to, patiently, and their answers waited for patiently. I must act as though they weren't here, with the knowing that they are. Here is the sky, sometimes blue, and here the churned mud of the field. Men lie where the light died in them. Here is a bush, poplar, its furred buds suddenly sprung like the tails of young lambs. This much, this is my country, I intend to die in it. There are no heroes, just mud and cold and the vanished.

Haworth

There is little enough to remember, the guitar's mouth, the sour taste of pennies. My neighbour told me her dream: she looked out of her window to see my furniture stacked in the yard and amongst it a coffin casually placed. I inked in the teeth on the photographs of all the presidents. I discovered how light from a dead star persists.

After the spread of husbandry by slashing and burning there was a decrease in the number of elms, their shoots eaten as pannage, and an increase in certain weeds, particularly mugwort and plantain. Working the earth men worshipped it as a mother, setting her eye to watch the dead in their long galleries and the white stones over them, each stone containing a new name for each handful of dust. After them came the metal workers who made a god of the fire at its source in the sun, burning their dead as was right for them, or crouching them as at birth.

We were countrymen, pagani, peasants, worshipping other gods than the dour guardians of the towns. In the cities we followed instructions, schedules, learning the new words for things. We studied a different history, forgetting the numbers of the battles, setting a crossed sword on the maps. The towns pushed back the forest. For each ship of the line 4000 oaks were cut down, casualties before the wars began. The builders turned to using green wood, so the bottom rotted out of the *Queen Charlotte* before she put to sea.

On gravestones the names of children thicken with lichen. I see that for my people sex was indeed death. My own time survives in a culture of death, the Greek officer on wooden stumps saluting the colonels and their flag. I am visited by dreams and solitudes and voices from lives not mine, poems full of the ghosts of other poems. June bugs batter the screens, their question *what is my life?* and the scarab answering *it is better to live*. So many things to be learned before the uselessness of knowing things, one cheer for all I am forgetting. The son carves a wooden image of his father's dead hand. It is from this he inherits his powers. I lie down to sleep, indifferent to what shore I shall arrive on. I labour to finish my house that my children may have shelter. At day's end I take a slate and write the word *satis*.

The wise administrator

We shall draw up lists of our needs, then of the things that will answer them. Whatever has been thought of is useful. What does not exist must be invented.

These are the secret things: a bowl of poppy seeds, the pupae hanging like bells from their twigs. Inside them unknown creatures are gnawing toward the light, the summer is waiting for them. On the walls are the scowled shells of horseshoe crabs, cat-tails and teazels, bird nests set in their branches, dried grasses of foxtail and bread wheat, an antler, a twisted root that describes the pirouette of a dancer. They are things discarded by their own worlds, filed here for future use, saved from oblivion that they may exist a little longer. If these things did not exist it would still be necessary to think of them. Without them I would be forced to go live among the damned.

The salamander: in the desert's heat its body turns to stone, it draws back into a single nerve the way God goes back into himself while man is doing his worst: the flesh dies, the spark remains, awaiting the coming of water. I shall leave my name, my date, the gestures of my hands and the movement in my face, the way my head cocks to one side, listening. I shall go away, needing these things only a while; you will point to them but I shall no longer be in them. You will be left with the lizard's tail across your hands, with the snake's fierce skin.

The makings

The sand dollar with its five wounds. These are the slits in the tower, too narrow to pass through, like the eye of the needle, defensive only. It is a shield that lives in protection of itself, a life reduced to that gesture. It withstands the sea's weight, sieves it all through five gills set like a star. A creature of the buried beaches, the ocean offers it up. Finding it I am consoled, I remember the battlements fallen out of use and the armour of pondering knights in the cathedrals. I see how guarded we are as we labour through the continents. Nothing can pass in but what we let. In such objects we find ourselves. Inside there are five small doves of bone, flying into each other.

The wild turkey

He worked for the language company, passing out words and phrases in the hope people would adopt them, as part of a complex marketing operation. If the words passing into currency led anyone to buy the products they stood for, he never knew. He trudged round the great estates and the districts of the city in all weathers for the chance of casual conversation into which he was supposed to drop the word of the week. Mostly he lugged home his briefcase not a sample lighter by the evening. Paid on results, the returns and the paycheques trailing months behind his efforts, he made some sort of living. It seemed the government, looking to language's impoverishment, were trying to restimulate it. He took the job, and stayed with it, there being nothing else. His work was to take out the packs of new vernacular and attempt to pass them on in shops and bars and public transport. It was a daft job, in which he aped spontaneity, trying to get the words across with just the right reserve of emphasis and understatement. What was sent him through the mail once a month was rarely memorable in any case. And he came not to want to be invisible, the monitor of someone else's words, neutral and disinterested. And yet what held him was the secrecy, and the paradoxes of his situation, there and yet not there, paid to move on. Only occasionally he met another agent, and once or twice a checker covering his tracks for words he'd left behind, and rarely he glimpsed the state poets commissioned surreptitiously through third parties and committees and dummy companies to write the stuff to be slipped into language at large by devious and largely ineffective routes, one of which was himself. Their work, he generally found, trod cautiously between blandness and violence, with surprises few, and by the time the labs processed their efforts all the great abstractions had been tidied up, all the words for love and grief so flattened out and set in general context as to make them meaningless. He came to see himself as ineffective, passing out words few could figure out a use for let alone adopt in conversation with a stranger. There was so little humour in it all. The bland mash of *nice beautiful the place's fault nights of September never brash then she took off leave it out, John* turned out to be what most people said anyway. And the checkers were known to be lazy. Therefore he would play, concluding that since all was vanity he may as well indulge his. The trick was to slip in words of his own from time to time, carefully, till the checkers noticed and figured out the source. After the reprimand they'd still remember him, and there might be some chance of promotion. He didn't particularly want to be a checker or an editor or even a state poet, but he reasoned he'd meet others like himself, querulous and wandering and mystified in all the strangeness, and even if they didn't meet they might be able to communicate through the words. He began slipping in words of his own making, in hope of doing so for as long as he might get away with it, in search of others like himself doing the same.

The man who could change things

You would say he hears only what he wants to hear. He's always inventing better circumstances for the mundane events of his life and the conditions he finds himself in – a series of personal fictions without much continuity. If the situation is not to his liking, attending the annual Friends of the Library buffet and cocktail party for example, he pretends he's an owl sitting in a beech tree in a great beechwood stretching from horizon to horizon as far as he might ever fly. He's nodding to the smalltalk around himself, but he's really an owl sitting in a tree nodding to some rustling in the bracken, the spring rain stiffening his feathers. This explains the predicament he finds himself in: he's an owl somehow delivered into the world of men and women through some bungle in the cosmic delivery service, and must endure the body and the life of the man he finds himself to be. I've asked him how he does it but all he ever says each time is *here comes the sky, it's blue; here comes the river, and it's blue too.*

In the south

A white metal country, the sun's light parching the grass, quickening the aspens. It is absorbed by nothing, its heat gathering above stones. The sea arrives gently, the way age and dignity want to be approached, wave after wave printing the beaches, white. *So this is the south* says the traveller, its glare all around him. Only the sky is true to its colour. In the well bottom a ring of water reflects darkness broken by an ellipse of blue and cloud crossed sometimes by birds. The bull groans from the fence, the chickens clack through the yard to the barn out of the heat, suspicion beneath each wing. In the cottages the vote is being counted: *one, one, one;* in the capital the crowd pushes up the street yelling *Vive Antoine*, and runs back yelling *À bas Antoine*. Those who take the tally always forget to count themselves in; there is no name on the ballot paper and there is only one candidate. Around here his name is spoken in secret, in whispers, in meetings where one man sits watching through the window, another through the door, while a third sits on the roof. No one is ever elected.

Second elegy

Other times the patterns will not form with any sort of order: the words of ordinary speech form into other messages in some unbidden language, other faces rise out of the moving screen made of the edges of stones and buildings, the perspectives altered around the arm of a chair, half a hill in the distance, the faces of people on the street, and the mind makes another order from it all. *No hump shunt* I read in chalk on the side of a goods truck on the outer assembly lines of York station. I can make no sense of that. *No hump shunt? Ubi sunt?* At such times I stay on the trains, and travel till the patterns change again to where what I see is merely cities and the landscape of wherever: barn, tree, telephone kiosk, the white towers at the edges of Birmingham amongst motorway and sunset, coils of wire in the locked yards, a man welding in the rain, the blue flash of his torch.

Clint's dream

There are four of them, one suburban couple entertaining another. They have eaten dinner, they have talked, smoked cigarettes and drank modestly. It is time for the visitors to leave. Outside there is a silence so blank they draw back from it. In the house they turn on the TV. On the screen there is nothing but a piano and a music stand. It is the same on all channels, and there is no break in the silence. Not knowing what to do they wait, watching the white screen until a voice from the set speaks to them: *you are the meek, you are the humble, you have inherited the earth.* And it is so; they are the only people left alive, and the world is theirs and theirs always, for the voice has told them they will not die.

For five years they enjoy the earth. All the cities are theirs to visit, all the mountains theirs to wonder at. They cross the Sahara, they track slowly through China, they explore the Amazon's brilliant darkness. There are times they grow weary of abundance: diamonds fall from their hands, they turn away from the Mona Lisa's endless smile, they give up the mystery of the labyrinth. At the last in a castle in Languedoc, they enter a high tower through its single metalled door. They mount the stone steps deeply grooved by the footsteps of centuries, at the top they look out over the landscape. Returning down the stone spiral they find the door locked against them. Nothing can move it. They cannot

40

open it. They are shut in without escape.

The voice returns, confirming their imprisonment. Yes: the world is theirs still; yes: they will live forever; yes: it is too bad they are imprisoned. They howl within the tower protesting that this was not what was promised. Before it is silent forever the voice answers them: *but I am not the God who made that promise.*

Passing bell

Far away now, so I no longer look for it at the ends of streets nor expect its white smoke to chill me nor feel its sound in me, the sea heaves at the edge of memory. The rock pool bristles with anemones, the sand with its flies and crabs and voices. The ocean has gone with its gulls and boats, ships settled under the horizon and their names silted out: *Pequod, Titanic, Orizaba.* I live far inland with people who have never seen it, the wave coming on taller than a man standing before it who remains when the wave has broken itself and gone back into the motion. Such people have the strange assurance of a cat who expects the world to sustain him, moving through the furniture and the grasses certain of himself in a world he's certain of. Only sometimes I remember it, the sea crying in the skull's white buildings, touching all the beaches with the same print, its grin narrowing around the continents.

Peyote summer

I sat down. I sat down and looked at the wall. The snake people came in and were dancing. The lizard people came in and were dancing. The doghead people came in and were dancing. All my brothers and sisters, all my sons and daughters, all my ancestors and descendants came in and were dancing. The land was covered in bilge and slime, old tanks rusting and fat-bellied animals moving sluggishly. At the bottom were huge insects with diamond faceted skins giving birth to more insects, huge, filthy, and others worse crawling out from between the diamond divisions. These grew larger, into animals, the dinosaurs, heaving great rocks from the sludge they waded in. The rocks were heaved up onto their shoulders, and piled there on top of each other, where they weathered,

41

cracking down into soil and sand, where plants grew in the world I saw myself alive in. Then was just a mass of vivid colours in thin writhing tubes of red and white and yellow and blue packed together threading in and out of the girl's skin. It was the same with my own. Later, thinking none of this unusual I went out to the woods behind the house. There I found a stick, bent over at the end where it had been broken as a young branch, the break the elongated shape of an animal head. The head was a wolf's mouth, and the tip of the jaw formed an eagle. Eagle born from the wolf's mouth.

The joined-up writing
(for BB)

I admit it then: my grown life an interruption of a childhood spent wandering in the Danelaw, and my dreaming skull. Always the sense of living another life elsewhere on the planet's side; perhaps sleeping I go there to my family and my work in the singing buildings, and all my dreams are the thin confused memories of that place as if seen underwater, a life beneath the long slope of the dale, amongst the sunlight and the elm trees. Awake what I do is mourn them, the great elms dying across the continents, and walk by the river in their vanished shadow. And then the rest: poverty chewing its nails all winter long, mixing charity's lemon juice with ashes for a starving man's supper, the rockets in their silos pointing straight to each other, the fact death happens once and forever to everyone, that I too will lie in the earth with a gauze napkin on my face and my hands folded like birds. How hard it is, just as you have described: the cart drawn up past midnight, the family packed. With a few neighbours they rope their goods to the cart and trundle off to see the dawn rise and the larks invisibly begin some other place, leaving their unpaid bills and dark farewells, and the corner shop's indignance. Amongst the jokes and the bars and the journeys and the love of good women, all the same I grow, as you grew years ago, 'weary of the autumn and the winter and the spring and summer too'.

The lovers unite

She goes to speak to the convention of mothers. Home again, she weeps as she tells him how they denounced her: Catholic bitch from Spoleto, Communist whore from Rega, Evangelical cow from Bruges, Protestant, Heretic, Fascist Jew-baiter from Bromley, Little Sister of the Fried Chicken. She weeps on his hands. In the supermarket she cannot rid herself of the conviction of her own nakedness, and stops to see if people are watching her, looking down to see her shoes, denim skirt, white blouse, tug and whisper of her underclothes, finding all present but unable to be rid of her sense of exposure. She weeps on his hands.

The exile's vision
(for Marek Laczynski)

Twice I saw her. Once, drilling my squad, tired from working for each man, exhausted in fact, I saw her at the edge of a wood waving to me. I was worn out, and the light thinning at day's end, but I saw her, clear as I see you. I went towards her, seeing a pretty girl in a thin white dress to her ankles, very pale, something about her that was blue. She vanished in front of me. There was nowhere she could have hidden. The second time was in Italy. We were moving through open country towards a hill, the ground very stoney. In the hillside we'd spotted a cave good for sleep or cover, but we were wary, on the lookout for enemy troops. So I was looking very carefully, everyone was, at the hill and the cavemouth. She was there, in the opening of the cave, the same girl, laughing: *oh the soldier, the soldier, the brave young boy*, and calling my name. I raised my sten and fired right through her. No one else saw her. They thought maybe I'd seen movement and been mistaken. But my eyes were good I tell you. I was trained to distinguish detail. The bullets went through and through where she stood. I never saw her again.

The night boat

Wherever it stops the ship will dock, there will be land and an open harbour. Sailing in, there are the sounds of water against the wooden keel, knockings, creakings of ropes, water lapping against itself. It is open day, the sunlight striking calm water, in the distance rain forming itself in a dark head of cloud. Black sails, black wood, the lights as on ebony, and around them clouds, gull cries, brown weeds, floating. On the boat and just around it it is night: a blackness in which the boat pitches, wherever it goes. There are shiplights before and aft, a dimmer light shines through the boat's windows. On deck a door is thrown open, the light casting outward is yellow, ancient. Where it spends itself pass dark bent figures, darker shapes of the light who if you could hear them would be muttering *Aleppo, Tangiers, Malacca*, over and over. A seaman, sitting in the prow, guides the boat to the quay; all that can be seen of him is the spark of his pipe that glows with his breathing, slow and even, the effort of an old man. When the boat is tied up they will roll the sails, they will open the hold and haul out their cargo, which is always darkness.

Ghost dancing at Wounded Knee

The Shoshone were back, and to the west the Northern and Southern Cheyenne reunited, and joined again with their brothers the Arapaho. The Apache, the Comanche, the Kiowa, the Chippewa, the Lakota and their enemies the Crow, and all the cruel and brilliant peoples of the plains. The Wasichi withdrew east along the border of the short grass prairie, their Bluecoats trailing through the dust-clouds covering the withdrawal. For the second but not the last time in history everything that had already happened happened again: the Cheyenne, Roman Nose, protected by a charm broken only if his food touched iron after being cooked, visited with a Lakota chief just before the battle of Beecher Island, discovering too late the food he was eating had been taken from the pot with an iron fork. Without enough time to go through the elaborate ritual necessary to renew the magic, he went into battle knowing he would die. He went reluctantly, urged by his brothers. *Hokaheyya: it is good day to die.* The prairie was again their own, with the horse nation and the buffalo nation, the tribes of the ants and the snakes.

It was said by all the bands of the Teton Lakota – the Brules, Hunkpapas, Two Kettles Band, the Blackfeet Sioux, Sans Arcs, Miniconjous and Ogalalas – and echoed up north by the Yankton and Yanktonai Lakota, and repeated among the Santee Lakota of Minnesota – the Sisseton, Wahpeton, Mdewakanton and Wahpekute – to be the work of the dancing begun by the Paiute, Wovoka, the woodcutter, who had a vision from God telling him to dance and sing and look within his hat and there he would see the nations renewed and their hoop unbroken. *Our world comes back*, they sang, *in the wing of the white eagle. The kestrel stands in the air.*

House-moving

I'm going home I said. But through which door, to what continent? My dreams fill with furniture – tables and chairs that must be shifted, eased through doorways too narrow for them. I wake with one corner of the dresser fixed in my mind and a dull pain from the wood's edge.

I would go home, but they are moving house again. There's no place to be there but hanging around the truck waiting for everything to just leave, the cats writhing in a bag, the teapot smashed. No place then but the distance and its attempt to be in one spot at a time, and our moving through it with chattels, tools, ornaments, crockery, stones from Vermont, Cape Cod shell, eucalyptus cone, objects encountered in transit. So there are all places: in one a brown fog over a river bank, in another a bird walking stiffly in a wet orchard, places of lost penknives, places where birds start suddenly from thick weeds, fields of golden-rod about to fade, the colour going from the high grass of the moorlands, in the coast towns the mist arriving. Otherwise there is the way we go, broad as daylight.

The morning of defeat

I have buried my dead and made my offering. I have been exorcised by salt and water. I own nothing but my sense of impermanence, that only. On dark nights when the town is sleeping I have found again the secret names of the intermediaries. I would wear my talisman of the moon, protector of travellers and exiles from shipwreck and madness. But the silver plaque is heavy, and where at this late hour will I get a diamond to engrave the crescent and the goblet and the name? We have lost the language in which to call and hold the darkness, and to curse our masters. There are no words of protection and immunity left. The damned stand naked before their owners, in their ashy flesh.

I make do with what I have, and offer this for a coin and talisman: the sand dollar of pure bone, stamped with the pentacle of the ocean.

Postscript from the Alpha Café

The truth is what I never said. I live most days far into the interior of this my life in this ageing body, its mind full of smoke and flickering video images. Clouds drift their shadows across fields in there, where I am with the birds turning in air, walking in the noonday city, in my head conducting my protracted personal war with the hostile civilisations in Andromeda. Coming away from that is never easy, arriving in my wandering flesh among the white Anglo-Saxon protestants in this sector in this fourth quarter of the twentieth century, however loud the music or lovely its women or fresh the air or bright the spring petals of the cherry trees. And then I must set to the work: counting the forks or explaining the workings of the turret grinding mill. And all for a few pounds so that I can go back into myself, where I am now, far away, with little enough desire to surface, and as the days pass there's less of a damned thing anyone can do to reach me.

The Wild Rose

John Patrick
1904-1971

I

Nothing to say for himself. After his death I learned what little there
is: born *Buncrana Inishowen Donegal*, 1904; name of father *Samuel;*
mother's name *Mary McGrory*. She died in his birth. He was sent to
England, to be raised by an uncle, a farmer, who didn't want him. He
worked. If he had any schooling it didn't show. He wrote his name in
a child's scrawl, claimed poor eyesight to avoid reading, refused eye-
glasses. My mother said when she met him he was carrying a suitcase
with two shirts in it. Nothing else. He said he was born in Northumber-
land, to have come from there, that his father's name was William.
Maybe he knew, or had never been told. Or maybe the clerks merely
tied up loose ends and matched two sets of papers to give me a life not
his. He never would talk of it. She remembered he would stare at a
knife and fork, not knowing which hand to take them in, when he came
into the house he said *goodnight* in greeting. She married him, his silence
and his violence and his gentleness. We went from farm to farm, a hired
man living in a tied house, the furniture piled in a cattle truck. His
fingers were frostbitten, white and stiff, I have spoken of them. Quarrel-
some, proud and private, he could agree with no one. Locked out of
one farm, he nailed every door and window to its jamb. Sacked from
another, he fired the stackyard. He had no friends, confided in no one,
his rhythm long quietness broken by bursts of sustained anger. It was
his solitude I loved; his stern face coming in from the frost, a stolen
chicken under his coat. And his shy grin, his slow walk through the
fields, the dog circling him. He did nothing but work, so long as there
was light to do it by, till the light went out of him, whatever it meant.

II

Dead. The pig with its throat cut and a steel spike through its forehead,
the chicken's neck broken, its wings still flapping, the poisoned cattle,
the horse died of anthrax, burned with the cart it lay on. We picked up
rabbits by their hind legs and snapped them with the sides of our hands.
Pups and kittens were put with a stone in a bag and dropped in the rain
barrel. At Christmas geese, turkeys, ducks, hung from the beams in
the wash-house, the air drifting with feathers. He left a long trail of
broken necks through the Ridings. He would spend cold nights out in

the field delivering sheep, guided by their cries and his stormlamp. I saw him cry for a dog killed on the road, he shovelled the muck into the pit after dead sheep. Kicked by horses, gored by bulls, he came back for more. There was no such word as *can't*. I looked through the window, saw him sitting in an empty room, the slaughtering knife in his right hand, the darkness in his face.

III

We lived on Sunk Island: flat and bleak. Canals, snakes, muskrats. The North Sea winds blew away everything. We had forgotten the sight of hills and trees.

An army tank came through the front wall of the house. He came home, cursing the driver. All of us were sick that winter. He got out of bed with pneumonia to prove he could work. We moved away.

He made Molotov cocktails in the yard, scaring the Italians. He preferred German prisoners, they worked hard. He fiddled with things that rarely turned out to be anything. Saved nails, rusty bolts, bits of tin, perspex, string. Believed in their usefulness.

Believed in work. To relax, he would stare into the fire, fall asleep. In summer in the late evenings sat in the yard staring at a leaf or a bird, fell asleep. Listened to the radio. On Sundays we'd dress up to take long walks, greeting our neighbours. We were never any place long enough to belong there.

He swept the table clean with one motion of his hand, threw back his chair and stomped out. Broke things, threw his dinner in the fireback. Fought, and complained of a hurt leg and forgot and limped on the other one. Suddenly angered, he broke the radio over my head. I have a scar by my right eye from him. It is old flesh now.

IV

Dead, then. The shy smile, the proud face. When the war came to an end he sat down with the prisoners. They were neither happy nor sad.

50

He put up flags to be seen from the road. I understood none of it.

Owning nothing, he dreamed of his own place where he would be apart, kept by his own word. Without place, he locked himself up in his rages, dumb. And worked; we worked, saved everything, went with necessity. In time he bought a store, then another. We lived in a city then, without horizons. The world closed on us. And went on working, dawn till dusk, all day and every day. I knew that without work he would die. He left off working and lived by the sea, six months. And he died.

I looked down into his face, put my hands on his, wanting to press back the warmth. I said aloud

> *the labour*
> *has dropped from your hands*
> *like stones*

V

I am back in the country I was born in. The East Riding is dour, they do not express much. The sky is grey, the grasses short on the small rounded hills. The Wolds are chalk and clay, good farmland going down to the sea, the mud cliffs falling in year by year.

Romans, Danes, Vikings. My people have nothing to say of themselves. The grey mists come in to settle. Our childhood must have been in another place, far away, where it is still going on. In the dusk we pretend to be aeroplanes, the bombers drone over our heads through the long fingers of light, the bombs fall on Hull. People are being killed all around us. We fall to the ground, but we rise again. I was hidden under a table and looked out to see flares falling across the road. I am afraid of the dark, and out there is nothing but darkness and misery, the stars fall through it forever. In a wood near us a plane came down. We would run to see the smokey pits they made, finding magnets and strips of twisted metal. That time in the wood I found a pair of good flying boots, inside them a pair of feet.

The great events follow each other. For the rest we live in the body, we occupy a space, we have a period of time, here where the generations have been before us. I cannot bear this silence, and I cannot return here.

VI

The dark surrounds us, we are pleased to see a little way into it. There are aficionados of the good death, those who choose hemlock or the asp or the bull stamping through the maze. But there are only the dead in their caves, with their cigarettes still burning in the ashtrays. The dead man trapped in the camera, his face still waiting to be developed. The dead man in the dark, luminous, flicking off/on like a crazy switch, and the seeds he planted in the garden growing after him. The dead in old movies, with their lights, with their black suits and scarves, with their voices saying *play it again Sam*.

The widows are nursing their hurts. It is all painful, even the joys hurt in the retelling. They walk through the long gardens, the weeping Maries and the crucifixions, marble and granite, names chiselled into them. The griefs continue, like a baby that will never grow up.

VII

I laboured to write this for him. The stone carries his name and dates and the middle name that may not be his, and a wild rose cut into its corner. There is another space, blank, waiting for the mallet.

The chalk folds around him, waits for the sea's coming. The silence has gone into itself. If the grave is that deep it is deeper.

I walk away from it, valuing my life, the woman I married, the children she brought out of herself crying. Months later I discovered I was happy, that my life meant it could not be given up. Whatever these are, whether they are poems or not, they are to celebrate, the drip of water building a tower of itself from the minerals it has gathered.

The dead lie with bitterness in their mouths. Something of them comes back, as he does, it does not disturb me. They want to go on, or to return to settle what was not done here; it is what holds them back, this wanting. I am happy that he chooses sometimes to be with me. I am his son; my house is his and I welcome him, wondering, since he was a private man who preferred silence and kept from his own kind, how he gets on with the other dead. Knowing we have made peace, he and I, I want him to make peace with them. They tower below us, like wheat.

Island called
Henry the Navigator

I, Fabricantes, poet and mapmaker, having spoken in a certain year with some of my ancestors, make these observations in answer to the questions put to me. We were till recently in the dark, knowing few shores. We lived like a needle floating on the skin of water, pulled towards the North Star as if yanked by the Devil's fingers. We were like mould in cheese thinking our colony and its neighbours the whole cheese cellar. Mawks in flesh were no wiser than us, chewing their side of a knuckle bone. We looked up to find ourselves on an inch of a six-foot corpse, scrambling for the way into the choicest eating. These notions were once new among us, at first senseless and refused as when the world was thought again to be round men argued that rain would fly upward, so still there are sailors who will not put out with the compass needle for they cry it is magic.

Men thought once that the Sea of Darkness would swallow them and bear them to the whirlpool at the world's end. Their ships hugged the land's sides, good seamen saw hidden rocks and shoals and knew distant headlands as they knew their own flesh, pointing through mists at the towers and distant lights. They feared the sea gods and the fogs and they durst not lose sight of land. It did not occur to them to go westward. What they desired lay east, in India and China and the Spice Islands: rubies, silk, pepper, cinnamon. No inhabited land lay beyond the Atlantic because no one had been there; no one had been there because there was nothing to go for. I don't know how many centuries we lived setting this contradiction before our fear of the great winds and the creatures we drew on maps. We clung to our corner of the planet, shut there to the mutual comfort of ourselves and others by our assuming that the known world was the world known to us. Sealed as we were we feared the dark contained nothing or worse. We kept our fields or raided our neighbours'.

I see an eye opening in the face of a sleeping man. He remembers nothing of his going to sleep and his sleeping appears to him only as he dreams. Of that other time when he merely slept he will remember nothing. He dreamed he was Roman, a captain marching his troops along some causeway. He sees the marsh and the reeds and the rabbits

54

vanishing behind white tails, like smokes. About a mile away a party of natives is watching them pass: the locals are shrunken and ragged, standing in silence. They are not holding weapons. He pays them no further attention and harries his soldiers. They are tough and suspicious, bearing the medallions of their own gods, tribesmen from another frontier who kill each other in brawls one moment and the next pick each other's nits, huddling together for warmth in their army issue. That was one dream. In each of his dreams he is oblivious of having had any other; the dream runs on, a little civilisation on its own, finding of whatever went before and survived it only a few ring-marked stones or the runes of some conqueror.

One eye has opened in the sleeper's face. He is not yet awake. He dreams he is the messenger of Darius come to Sparta to demand earth and water. He knows their reputation: the Spartans are bacteria. Where he stopped for rest they laughed in his face and ran from him as a man going to his death. *Sparta* they yelled back *will give you a pension good as Homer's and you as blind will deserve it. Of earth and water they will give you piss and shit.* Sparta was a hive of bees camped on the plain. Or Sparta was a fighting crab stationed on the ocean's floor. They threw him down a well with earth and water enough. In most of his dreams he has no distinction whatever: peasant, soldier, fishwife, slave, seaman; his dreams are of labour and submission. He dreamed he was a monk tending the silence of his order, sailing with his companions in the stone ship of the monastery, adrift on the centuries. That silence overpowered his life: it was the endless silence of the universe he heard, imagining himself cupped to the mouth of God that never spoke.

He hears the sounds of the world, its changing light falls on his face, the waking dream is more vivid. As he begins to realise *it is a world* he shifts it into his dream. He hears the sound of traffic on the highway, it is the millwheel he is listening to. He is standing in the wooden mill where the shafts and belts and gears run through the walls from room to room. The water races outside and the paddles scrape along with it; beneath his feet the grinding of the great stones rattles all the building. He is used to it, and to the silk sheen of the crushed meal on his skin,

55

its oiliness. He need not go hungry for there is always a handful he might take for himself. In this life he is a miller, bent under grain. The mill ceases, its timbers rot and the milldam breaks. The millstones found among nettles are taken to be set in the side of a house. He dreams of his dying, the smile flying from his face. He lies down with the newly dead.

They are everywhere, the dead, laid east to west as is our custom, like the spears of an army just under the earth, like millions of needles. The corner of a house speaks of the man who leaned there of an evening when he'd done working. Other images clutter in: boxes of new shoes, packed skulls in the crypts of Sicilian churches, a rack of cut logs, the lanyards threaded through a deadeye. They are the past: us dreaming who we will become. The dead hand their names over to the desk clerk who hangs them on the key hooks; most names are let out again, others like Caesar Augustus and Odysseus are reserved for special occasions in the future. Names like Judas Iscariot and Attila the Hun will never be used again for anyone. They are packed in dozens in the cellar or put under glass. So much I know of the dead; they are dead but they are not contented.

I have decided to take stock. For centuries the Chinese guarded the secret of the silkworm and Mohammedan traders brought silks and spices overland, keeping the secret of where they went over the long plains. Business men are like that; the Phoenicians drew maps deliberately placing the Tin Islands far out in the Atlantic where the Greeks would not find them. The Greeks did not find them. As we set out beyond Cape Non will anyone greet us? Travellers bear letters to distant kings who do not know our languages: do they too have words for ignorance and darkness and water?

Henry the Navigator, Prince of Portugal, built a tower to house his observatory and school of navigation. From all Europe he brought instruments and charts, accounts of voyages, geographers, map makers, sea captains, setting them to the single purpose of his life: to find the way round Africa to the Indies. For 40 years he urged frightened sailors beyond new capes and watched the craggy African coastline nudge southward on his maps. He died before Bartholomeu Diaz rounded the Cape of Storms. In another ten years the Portuguese under Vasco da Gama again rounded the cape, finding the ports on the northern landfall. From there they were taken to India: the route was opened. Finding it they had measured Africa as though with a rope. Meanwhile, sniffing the winds for spices, Columbus stumbled on that other continent, the third corner of the iron triangle. The voyages of Diaz, Columbus and da Gama happened within a period of ten years. The Europeans prayed to their god to favour them; all men assumed his interest in their greed. Asked what he looked for in India da Gama answered 'Christians and spices'. Spain, for whom Columbus had claimed a few useless islands beyond the western sea, was disappointed. Columbus died not knowing what he had found. Ferdinand ended his days grumbling at the expense, remembering the stories told on the return, how Columbus holding aloft cross and flag and carrying letters to the King of Cathay had met brown skinned natives whom he assumed to be inhabitants of islands off the coast of China. They stared at him, hearing his strange language. He called them Indians, they said *no those folks are much further we are called people.*

For a perspective of history read as fiction. When we got there we found China superior: there was nothing they wanted of us. Later they bought sage from the Dutch at a great price and later still the opium poppy. We were driven by avarice, working for cunning princes jealous of each other. In our own lands we cured sickness with charms and mumblings, set curses under our neighbours' doorstones. Kings plotted each other's deaths by knives and poison and sorcery. Much has survived of the old magic of the tribes, those who had broken before the Roman phalanxes, and those who came after. Whether the old cures worked or not they were stamped out. While the captains crept around Africa and out into the Atlantic witches and heretics were burning all over Europe; eight years before Columbus stepped onto the beaches of the New World Pope Innocent VIII issued the Bull that began the Inquisition. The Inquisitors ground out the old beliefs, cures and curses, wheat before the millstone: Europe waking dreamed more vividly before daylight.

On the royal contract of approval for Columbus' expedition to the Indies: April 17, 1492. On the royal edict driving all believing Jews from the Spanish Kingdom within three months: April 30, 1492. The Sephardim were being fleeced and herded to the frontiers of Castile and Aragon as the Genoan put to sea. The same men carrying flags and letters across the earth like images travelling out of that opening eye were superstitious sailors who might not take a woman aboard ship for fear she carried the devil in her, though were she black it did not matter. Sailors becalmed in harbour might send to buy a rope knotted three times: unfastened, one knot let out a breeze, another a gale, the third a hurricane. These men gaped at the blue waters of the Pacific. What might the Great Khan have said to them – swaggering ashore with their bottomless thirsts and their strange curses? Imagine the Chinese bringing the maxims of Confucius along the Via Appia, confronted at dawn by grave robbers, old soldiers darkened by the worship of Roman Mithras.

Those asked to complete the questionnaire on freedom were instructed to answer all questions; those unwilling to answer all the questions were expected to state their reasons in the space provided. This is called a nil return. I checked the box marked 'registered anarchist' and attached my non-affiliations. The twelve questions looked up at me, I felt free to answer them and began *I, Fabricantes, in the 34th year of my time on earth, greet you. I have conversed with the fleas on the dog's back and they told me their sciences and the names of their planet, but I am without influence and it is too late to warn anyone. I had a father who was a judge but was impeached for perjury and taking bribes. I had a father who was a duke but he was deposed. I had a father who was an ambassador but in the revolution he fell from favour. I had a father who was something in the church but he stood in error. I had a father in the security force but he died fighting the whorehouse fire which is where my mother went on dying. It would make no difference if a stone were my father. And anyway that was among the Brigantes where I was born though they are no more my people than the wind is. When they say I was one of them and owe them duty I reply yes and I was born in a snowstorm in the early morning but I pay no taxes to winter and I am not asked to die in the name of 5.00 a.m.; I was born in December but I did not take its name.*

The last trial and execution for witchcraft in Western Europe happened in 1782 at Glaris in Switzerland. Not long before this prosecutions had taken place to repress the 'terrible and formidable' sect, the Illuminati. Amongst those accused were boys of 12 and 14 and a girl of 9 with her sister, younger than she. The civilisations of the Incas and the Mayas were long gone by then, Africa's kingdoms dismantled to cram slave ships, and the heathen butchered in the name of Jesus, last known as the Son of God. The sleeper is awake now and steps about his world with ease. He disdains the sleep he woke from and the dreams he endured, he assumes his right to the world and to spread his version of the light around it. He is awake but he is mad. He wakes the other sleepers, making some mad as himself, murdering some, hearing no one. When he looks into the mirror the man sees himself: awake, proud, triumphant – but the image of a lie is a lie, parting its hair on the other side. He lies down among the dead and addresses his god: he says *we woke to discover ourselves on this world and took possession of it* and his god replies *perhaps it has merely suited me to imagine a world of creatures slowly finding themselves its inhabitants, but now that they have felt their way around it and leave footprints on the moon I say so what. Perhaps it has suited me that in that dream they imagine me pretending they exist.*

And this is my tribute to the gods of explanations and questions, though I am sick of repeating myself. I am tired of being mad amongst the mad and tired of being a sack with arms going about filling itself and shitting. At the next to last question I baulked and wrote that Columbus sailed clear across Atlantic and Pacific together, there being but one ocean and no continent between, but finding no spices he invented other islands on his way across the western sea. How else might he justify the cost and raise money for another expedition? Years later with the Portuguese in India the Spaniards discovered Columbus's bluff but maintained it for it brought the bankers running from all over Europe hot for tales of cities of gold and crystal. Cultures were invented or transformed to suit the mythical Americas: a fantasy dreamed by Europe, America stimulated the slave trade and the gold trade and currency speculations, it was a place to send the excess populations who were shipped out only to arrive unknowing back in their destinations just as a man approaching a familiar street from the other direction does not recognise it as his own. When the English crushed the Scots and dispersed the clans the migrants were taken off in boats and dumped in the ocean. Those few who got through were circled around the ocean and brought back: *och* they said *it looks like home*, they called it Nova Scotia. Whatever America is it is not in the western sea where the eastern missiles are homed but I do not think we should tell the Great Khan and the wild men of the steppes.

Anus mundi

September 5, 1942

This afternoon present at a Sonderaktion from the women's camp. Horrible. Captain Thilo, the troops' doctor, was right this morning when he said to me we're at anus mundi. *In the evening about 8 o'clock again present at a Sonderaktion from the Netherlands. The men want to take part in the actions for the special rations they get for it – a fifth of a litre of schnapps, five cigarettes, a hundred grammes of sausage and bread.*
Today and tomorrow on duty.

– From the diary of Dr Hans Hermann Kremer, Professor of Medicine at the University of Munster and member of the Waffen SS, on secondment to Auschwitz.

The Kommandant

I was trapped, you see. Orders came, I carried them out. It was hard work. I was always occupied with one project or another, my wife urging me to relax. While my superiors pressed more work upon me I was criticised for not socialising with my subordinates and attacked for not delegating authority. And so I was torn from all sides; I felt like a man beset by wolves. Invariably the omissions and mistakes of my subordinates set me in a flap, I was forever foraging for building materials and kitchen supplies, and what with the chaos and shortages of wartime I was kept busy. It was make do and mend and shift for yourself all the way. So I was always sidetracked, I could not concern myself with how the place was run day to day, though I saw enough to know it was run badly. There was little I could do about it. A commander cannot bury himself in details, he cannot check that his directions are carried out. He must concern himself with overall policies, this is what I tried to do. It was not my fault the duties and functions I delegated to others were not carried out.

But the difference in me was noticeable. Sometimes I took relief in alcohol, never so much as to become drunk you understand, but sufficient to release me from my normal quiet. At such times, though these occasions were few and far between, I ceased to be so inward. But my reponsibilities were always upon me. I must constantly set an example to others. Distressed as I was by the brutalities that went on beneath me there was little I could do to alleviate them. My orders were usually 'reinterpreted', I was continually sent men of the wrong type: brutes, men without soul or intelligence whose only method was naked cruelty. And the intrigues that went on! It is surprising to me now that men so lacking in subtlety with their relations with others could employ such extraordinary complexity in order to trap each other and so gain some small advantage. Prisoners and guards were alike in cunning and depravity.

I shiver now to think of those years: nothing but hard work and no thanks, nothing but backbiting and complaints. That I should have been so unlucky in my inferiors was a continual misery to me. And so it went on: everyone jockeying beneath me, a daily routine of humiliation, brutality, profiteering, chicanery. Believe me I have had ample opportunity to observe that man is the most callous and the most cunning of creatures. In prison his true self steps out: he will steal from the dead, he will steal from the dying; weakness is merely to be exploited; malice, greed, dominate his every thought, he can advance only by the fall of others, he survives in the death of his comrades. As for those wretches unable to beat or bribe their way into positions of influence, they simply died as they sank. And my problem was to watch their torment while still trying to do my job, unable to improve their lot and being made to rub my nose day after day in the human animal. Disgusting. I have been sickened by all of this. Love, kindness, humanity, these are nothing but masks.

Monuments

I dreamed the murderers came to raise monuments over the dead. They brought with them flowers and small gifts. For all the teeth knocked out they raised a great stone molar, for all the bullets a single stone bullet. In the likeness of each living thing they had broken they put up a memorial: for the broken noses, for the busted skulls, for the crushed genitals. Lastly, and taller than all else in that field, they had unveiled a great stone finger.

Before the stones they protested: it was not so, it was not this way but this way. Pointing to each other they pointed to another who had done worse. It turned out that each of them had been too powerful to have noticed mundane suffering or not powerful enough to have done anything about it. They had obeyed orders, they were cogs. The one who had given the order was always elsewhere, perhaps gathering wildflowers for a memento. Or perhaps he was standing by some monument having his picture taken for a keepsake, or contemplating the most appropriate form of an immortelle for his victims. There was always another who had exceeded, had killed more, destroyed more. Soon they were arguing figures and economics and history and personal affairs; soon enough it was clear that however many had died no one had killed them. I was alone then, crying out of sleep: *but I am not consoled.*

In the bar

Franz knocks over his glass, he is drunk again. *Salud!* The beer runs over the table. Franz laughs. Before anyone can move it has soaked their pants and run down into their boots. They sit, protesting it's all right, pulling the wet cloth away from their crotches and thighs. Franz calls the waiter, someone buys another round. Every morning Franz is out of bed at dawn. First thing he shaves, singing through the foam into the mirror, a yelping that starts somewhere low in his belly and, as it rises through his chest and throat, gathers harsh resonances. The more face he shaves the quieter he becomes. When he's done, his voice, having sunk down through all available octaves into a quiet hum, has become a faint breathing. Holding the mirror he stares into his reflection, the dark lines under the eyes and around the mouth, the ever-receding hairline. He is silent a while before he snarls into the image of his scowl the syllables *bastard*. Poor Franz, he has never known peace. He fought first in the Middle East, then in Turkey. It's said he wept when he first killed a man. Along with the rest of his unit he refused to surrender after the war. They came the long way back through Russia. After that he enlisted again and served in the Baltic, guarding the frontier. He was a factory guard and a courier for various organisations. Those events seem strange now, far away, as though they'd happened in another time, on another continent, the moon perhaps. The war came again, Franz fought again. Now there's no more fighting to do, no more prison. Franz has no uniform and no instructions: a man surviving into other times he can't cope with. Sometimes, very drunk, he will tell of the East. Apart from the business of shaving, it's the only time he speaks in a whisper.

Joseph

The work. Sometimes I think I will never be finished. Impossible, my mind says, to clean every bed of its bugs. But I go on: speeches, travel, planning, writing. And the work yet to be done: all the scribblers to be organised into their colonies, all the painters and playwrights and slogan writers to be encouraged in the right way, all the verbs, nouns, participles, to be filed for easy reference and their case histories in easy reach. It must be done, I have said so many times.

For relaxation I have conceived an impossible task: the *Black Sonnets*. Can anyone else know my feelings, my sentiments, in the matter? I would like to think that someone coming after me will do it, someone with the genius of a Goethe or a Shakespeare, someone with both the insight and the discipline to read my heart. I'd tell him, listening up there in the future, what he would then embellish and repeat: I obeyed, I gave her up, the Czech woman. So there you are my hypothetical friend, born long after my time, the poet of the *Black Sonnets*. I gave her up. I saw her pale smile and silently wished her well. My last words to her: *bleib wie du bist*. Stay as you are, I cannot bear to think of you changing. Stay with my print on you, as you are, as you were, so remain; be always as you were for me.

But the *Black Sonnets!* Impossible.

The wings

In the third month the shoulder blades began to bud. Within another month the small wings had pressed themselves through the flesh: delicately stretched tissues, webbed and graceful, their planes and arcs speaking gently to us. The beatings, the hunger, the loss of all possessions, of homes and names and kin – was it for this so many had died? As the wings grew the guards softened, punishments were fewer, and when there were beatings the guards carefully avoided these marvellous growths on the shoulders, praising their beauty even as they laid on the whips. As the wings grew stronger the authorities withdrew to the perimeter. All but essential work ceased, roll-calls became perfunctory. Sworn to secrecy, eminent doctors came to examine the wings, pressing the delicate formations with tentative fingers and stainless steel instruments, measuring, making notes. Officials came from far away to inspect. Evidently the development was a mystery to all of them. They shook their heads often, but said nothing to us. The food improved, especially we noticed more calcium in the diet. We began to dream of escape: of flying.

It was not so. When the wings had grown and everywhere branched out glistening and shimmering in the winter sunlight, and when the agreed day for flight had arrived, the wings proved useless. We ran about hopelessly, like chickens, beating our great wings, unable to leave the ground. The wings were mere ornaments. The guards returned kicking and screaming to break the wings with their bare hands.

The winter of 1941

Water froze in the taps, we could not break the solid ice in the well and must go to the river to collect chunks of ice. We cut up furniture for fuel. Each week more people were taken away, the only relief from the food shortage. Since October the peasants had been prevented from coming into town to sell produce. What crops they had managed to gather had gone to the army, there was nothing left for us. Later we learned it had been official policy we should starve. People devoured what they could: horses, dogs, cats. At night I secretly ate mouthfuls of straw from my mattress, forcing into my belly a taste of age and sweat with nothing of the smell of cornfields in it. I thought of all the feet whose dirt had sifted down into that straw, of all those born and died on that mattress, the copulating, the cries, the sickness endured there. I thought: *the leavings of other lives, men and women and children, I am eating.* Then the snow came, falling everywhere. In the town we could get about, but we could no longer dodge the patrols and go to the countryside to look for food. Out there the peasants huddled under the snow, devouring whatever they had hoarded. The snow went on falling, filling the roads, covering everything, and froze solid. It seemed it would never go away, and across its miserable back the troops still came: trucks, tanks, marching columns headed further east, wherever the war had got itself to.

Eva

Publicly he would say *did you sleep well my dear?* Sometimes I would want to go home, I would want to go back to my people. He would not hear of it. Well, I had everything, the dancing, the social gatherings, receptions, the interminable evenings of Wagner. But he never said *I love you Eva.* I might appear at his side for the photograph, I might sit beside him or be introduced down the line of foreign bigshots. You could tell what they thought, those people, always fussing round him, paying him endless attention, listening to his rambling and reminiscences and laughing at the same jokes over and over as if they'd never heard them before. Gerda, Magda, their heads were high enough, whatever was said about them, they knew who they were. Even his dog was better off than I, at least it was *his dog, the dog.* I was just *Eva, Miss Braun, Eva Braun.* I was just my name.

Heinrich

What next, now I have killed everyone? First that crude queer Roehm and his boys, the waiters, bartenders, the innkeeper. The bad actors and the useless salesmen and the failed dramatists, the whole riffraff. Those with imperfections: wooden legs, false eyebrows, the myopic, the dumb, the daft, the shopkeepers cheating on the weights. Then the abnormal and the inferior races: the black, the white, the scapegoats, the albinos, the incestuous villagers of the mountains, the speakers of foreign tongues and those who merely count beans in the beanfield, the crazy professors. All gone, down to the last pimply office boy. I strangled the portraits on the walls, ripped out the testimonials, smashed my feet into the icons, liquidated the marble statues, the plaster casts of Byron and Adonis. Cleared out: Europe, clean as a whistle. My files are complete, the offices working to full capacity. Now we will catalogue the achievements of dead cultures, we will recognise value – wherever it existed. Like the Chassidim I shall find some good. Meanwhile, I spread my hands, I look into my reflection in my private mirror. I stare solemnly back at me.

Hermann

In the evening they lit a huge bonfire and gathered round it singing. I was exhausted from the speeches and the marching, and yet those faces about me shone with such radiance in the firelight I could not have thought of leaving though my official attendance was over. And the music that poured from the sweet throats of those young men and women! They sang of the mountains and rivers, of the great past and of the great future to come. I felt inspired. The speeches, the flags and the uniforms and the firm resolution everywhere manifested, all this made more potent by the sheer joy in those young faces, the energy of their voices and the starkly resolute looks in their eyes. How might we ever die? Soon I was singing with them. A young girl, one of the finest specimens in the gathering, took a brand from the fire and came up to me, holding the flame behind and above me so my face stood in the light. The crowd turned to me as we stood and sang together. I knew that my face as I sang would be illumined, a shifting map of shadow and light, and I thought of the light falling across our country, light and dark, light and dark – the plains, the forests, the valleys, the long shadows of the mountains. This was pageantry, the return of the old days though we sang of our future; we blended the memory of Frederick with the coming of Siegfried. It was then the tears burst for utter joy from me.

From the diary of Chaim the chemist

Bottles, jars full of liquids: green, blue, red, a yellow like urine. The large orange letters are ornate, from another century: they spell *shame, guilt, misery*. Their acids eat through, there is nothing that withstands them forever. They corrode wherever they touch.

Slow diminution: the glaciers come down, the ice melts, it finds the sea. The rocks slowly dissolve, even the gneiss, the granite, even the mountains, they are washed out in streams of silt and crystal. The lake fills with poisons, turns sluggish, or evaporates. Even the sea dies. But pain never lessens. Whatever happens has always happened, is part of our knowing. We are what happened to us. Guilt never diminishes, it remains, indissoluble, a lump no alkaloids will change; it devours everything but itself. There are no ovens to burn it to ashes. Dig it up, it has stained the ground, the soil is faint green.

And no innocent bystanders, even amongst the unborn. And no language sufficient to it, no words not corroded by our persecutors. They drag us down even in our words for suffering. And there can be no forgiveness, we cannot beg that from the victims. Yet while the victim cannot forgive, his persecutor cannot be redeemed – and so long as there is no redemption how shall we be delivered from persecution? It's a pickle in a narrow necked pickle jar.

I write that someone may know who we are, and I am no innocent. I would pray, but suffering has rendered God redundant. Who would I pray to?

Hans

In my dreams I see the mountains and the sky and I am freed of that other person, the one I was. Though that man is also myself, though I said all I said and I am not going to claim now that my conduct then was under pressure of circumstance, nevertheless I am deeply mystified. It is strange to me that I can be these two: the Hans who undertook the work he elected to do, who saw himself as some medieval vassal overlord, and yet that I can also be the Hans who sits here regretting all of it. It's as if I suddenly discovered myself in my own reflection, as if I had stepped out unexpectedly from the mirror. Very strange. Well, I am not going to be hypocritical; the only pity I would feel, all I would allow myself to feel, was for the shining blood of the German people. It was on their behalf that I spoke and acted here, and if my command was often confusing I saw distinctly that within my own sphere I was the embodiment of justice. I worked within my own jurisdiction in so far as it was clear to me: my mission was the Führer's, his destiny Germany's and my own, as it turned out a black destiny. Poles of course were another matter. Charged with maintaining law and order I put down all opposition ruthlessly while with my other hand I showed the velvet glove. I insisted that all who might resolve themselves into leadership be immediately snuffed out. We were not out to convert the Poles. Strange now to look at what I wrote and said then; it's like seeing another person in action and only then observing that his voice and face and mannerisms are one's own, that this person is oneself. It's like an aria to which one listens intensely, taken over completely by the splendour of the music and the irresistible grandeur of the voice and of the emotions; the melody enraptures and in the echoes of its close you give yourself to the applause. Tumultous, one says, tremendous. And then afterwards, alone, you think: it wasn't really so good, how could I have been so deeply moved? One feels foolish, to have given away so much of oneself. And yet it was so. *It is interesting to observe one's own reactions.* Thinking back I see now how mesmerised we all were, eighty million marching to the same step, crying the same cry. You know I was told once, by an old teacher of mine, to stay out of it: 'Political movements that begin in the criminal courts will end in the criminal courts.' That's what he told me. So here I am, too late the wiser. And yet, though I can see how ridiculous all that was, I stretch out my hand sometimes as though it were all here again. I see how simple it was. We were seduced, you see, like women falling at the feet of their conquerors. That man's voice reached down into each of us, demanding to know who we were at the very centre of our being – a place that exists beyond our names and the superficialities of identity – it struck into us where all our several desires intersected lifting them to an apex of longing. It demanded of each of us absolute submission, complete obedience. And we were glad to give it: that voice promised a world made new, a world we would renew – at whatever cost. And we knew there must be sacrifices. We saw the first tangible fruits, and seeing them we accepted, and accepting were lost forever. Look, sometime, into those eyes; there are no secrets from eyes like that, there is no denying whatever they demand. That man's eyes penetrate into the furthest crannies; they understand the darknesses, the desolations within us.

Boxes

They stand one on another, one by the other. They are all equal, perfect cubes made to stack up, their dimensions arranged to fit ship, truck, aeroplane, warehouse, and no loose space left. They contain everything: corpses, documents in evidence, broken glass, the secret poems of adolescents. They are addressed to Moscow, Detroit, Vienna, Calcutta; wherever there is a place with a name it has a means of receiving them, they will arrive: boxes of crockery, paper plates, propellers, howitzers, the loot from galleries and museums. How can it be that everything is made to fit them? It is easy, say the boxes, ask nothing; take it easy. The song of the boxes: we contain, we conceal, whatever you know, whatever you don't know. There is nothing but to be filled or be empty. Populating the long sheds, each of them may be thought of as *The Perfect Box*, the ideal from which all the others derive. Or they may be thought to contain mountain water, a spring breeze bringing thistledown and the breath of marigolds, a wooded slope busy with the throaty calling of pigeons, a Tyrolean landscape.

Captain Glück

I have now accepted the possibility that I shall lose everything. Once, when all this began, I was afraid. Afraid of death, afraid of being wounded, especially of being blinded or crippled or emasculated. Since then I have seen too much to be afraid any more. Should I be terribly wounded I shall simply ask a comrade to finish me off. I would not care to linger in agony. Should I be in a situation where capture by the Russians is inevitable, I shall shoot myself. Once I saw myself as the crippled Italian officer in the Hemingway book saying *a man should not put himself in a position to lose*. Now I see there is no choice in the matter and I am free of such romantic notions. Whether I want to or not I shall go on fighting, I shall do my duty. The only separate peace to be made is with death. There is no such thing as choice. And so I have resolved the possibility, the probability, of losing everything. I look upon each day now as the last and enjoy it the more. And strangely, taking all kinds of risk, I lead a charmed life. The other worries of soldiers do not touch me. That my wife will be unfaithful in my absence I regard as very likely, an event no doubt by now accomplished many times. I heard of a man, an officer killed at the front, whose wife in his absence began an affair with a French prisoner. Later the prisoner escaped, went to Berlin where he lived with the woman and paraded around in the husband's uniform. When the husband was killed the Frenchman, who spoke good German, merely assumed his identity. He was unmasked by an officer on leave from the same regiment. Another woman, the wife of an officer in my own unit, was a woman of liberal pretensions. Before his enlistment she persuaded her husband to take in a Jew, a former friend of the family. They hid him in their apartment, fed him and kept the police away. Later, when the officer had been sent to Belgium, he returned on leave to find his wife sleeping with the Jew. I have nothing against Jews, but I wish that one no luck. Such things do not worry me personally; I shall lose my wife, most likely to some miserable shirker clever enough to stay out of action. I shall lose my children in the bombing. I myself will be killed.

A corporal of infantry

I'm tired and I'm cold and my foot hurts, that's all I know. It's quiet now, we sleep, talk, play cards, sleep. We steal chickens and potatoes, we eat well. But I wish it was over. I can think of better things to do and I can think of better ways to fight a war. Suppose they just fought with snowballs or cream pies or paper weapons. The supply problem would be simpler. I'd like to see the paper planes coming over, shooting them down with slingshots. Or they could spend all the money on food and invite the other side over and feed them till they couldn't move and then take them prisoner. Or challenge the other side to drinking till one side or the other is dead drunk. Or suppose they had whole armies of marching bands. I could learn to play a trumpet just as well as I learned to shoot a rifle. Dismantle it, clean it, bull it till it blinds you, reassemble. All by numbers. Then playing the thing, marching drill, *present instruments*, all that. It would be just the same except we wouldn't get killed. The armies could meet in battle and try to outplay each other. The officers would all be conductors. The side that gets tired out first or runs out of tunes is the loser. Imagine: there'd be little skirmishes with the flutes and ambushes by the strings and big frontal attacks with the brass blaring and drummers booming. There'd be sneak attacks – musical patrols out trying to trick the other side into playing in the wrong key or missing the beat. And spies in there sabotaging the turns and counterturns, slipping in a wrong note, messing up the footwork, sucking lemons. They could suddenly slip in a few bars of a swing tune when the enemy is playing an overture. Or one side might play very slow and solemn trying to undermine the other while they're playing a rousing march. Beethoven versus Vera Lynn. Psychological warfare. It could all be a lot more interesting. Reiner says that in the first one he heard of a section of the line where they put up screens and showed dirty movies to the other side, trying to catch them off guard. Think about that, both sides trying to outdo each other. Finally one lot or the other would be so demoralised they'd be jerking off the whole time and they'd be decimated sneaking off to get laid. Maybe both sides would just desert and go home to their girlfriends. Think of a war fought with dirty jokes: you have loudspeakers and have to tell the other side jokes till they split laughing. Or how about this one – the women have to join up too and when the war starts you get to fuck all the women on the other side, as many as you like. The winner is the last side left with a hard-on.

The forest talking

The trees are full of spent bullets. Under the leaves are landmines and hidden guns. People come by, usually very slow and quiet, they make themselves move this way till they do it naturally like deer or rabbit, listening. They live deep in and come out either to take food from the villages or to attack others whom they kill, even the wounded. Others come by road, in trucks. They also take food from the villages. Sometimes they take and kill people from the villages and burn their houses. Sometimes they hunt the people in the woods and try to kill them or are killed by them. Sometimes the people in the woods kill the villagers, sometimes they kill each other. They all fight, even the villagers. Sometimes after fighting side by side against the people on the roads the people of the forest fight among themselves. And there are others, wanderers, who have neither guns nor food. They usually die, killed by the villagers or the road people or the forest people. People without guns or food come through every day on the railway, crammed into wagons, locked in and guarded. They never come back. The trains that return are either empty or filled with shoes, underclothes, hair. Some of the people on the trains get out and wander in the forest eating berries and roots before they die. Some of the forest people kill them, others take them in and together they fight against the road people. By the track there are bodies, thin and ragged. Also there are suitcases, tin cans, bottles, photographs, documents and passports and sometimes money the villagers pick up though there is nowhere they can spend it.

A victim

He had been working all morning carrying buckets of clay from the diggers to the carts. The carts could have been brought nearer, but then he would have had other work, equally hard, to be done on the double, digging the clay or pushing the loaded carts. The sun beat down on him, the sweat ran out over what was left of him. His body was running out of itself. The wooden shoes cut into his already cut feet, the sores on his back chafed, he ached in every cell. He had long ceased wondering how he did the work, and simply did it, not seeing the others, seeing only buckets, clay, carts, the path from the face to the carts and back again. Also he saw guards and the foreman. Twice already the foreman had struck him, once across the cheek, once across the back. In his universe of pain the blows meant no more than flies' bites to a horse.

But he was slowing down, he knew it. The foreman screamed at him and struck him again several times. Then the sergeant, Muller, came up: *what's wrong with this man?* The prisoner stopped, still holding the two heavy buckets of clay. The sergeant looked steadily at him, a questioning look. *I have a rupture,* the man said, *it was healed but now it is beginning again. From an operation, a few years ago.* The sergeant wanted to know what kind of operation. It was a general operation on the stomach, a laparectomy, exploratory. *Interesting.* Muller pitched his head forward a little, almost like a bird. *Show me,* he said, his voice all sympathy, quiet and interested. The man put down the buckets and opened his jacket, then, seeing the scar went on down below his belt, opened that and the fly of his trousers. He stood holding up his pants, Muller inspecting the long red scar and the swelling beneath it. Muller stepped back. *An operation, huh?* his mouth said, the sweetness hardening as the words came out. *And what would you like now, a month in hospital perhaps? Or light duties? Would that put you right? I can fix it.* The voice was pitched now, a hard shrill. *You shit, you shitty Pole. Maybe you'd like the Nobel Prize?* As he spoke he was stepping back, the voice rising to a scream; he swung his boot full force into the man's stomach. The man pitched over, his trousers tangled around his ankles, he rolled on the ground. Muller kicked the man again and again till he was dead. He turned to the foreman? *See, this man was ill, I have given him emergency treatment. But the shitty bastard shat himself and died of his own stink.*

The good soldier

At Rovno there was more work, the same as in Slonim and Minsk and Kiev and the other towns we'd been in. We rounded everyone up for processing: Jews, communists, politicals, intellectuals, queers. Most of them went easily enough. We told them they were to be shipped east, there'd be work for them there and places to live. Most of them believed us, or preferred to. Some of them barricaded themselves in or hid so we had to dig them out. It was soon clear to them what was going on. Others came out yelling and kicking, hitting with anything they could get their hands on – planks, knives, and some with guns. We smoked

75

them all out and shot the lot. There was some engineer trying to rescue his workmen, a bunch of Jews. Being a civilian he made a pest of himself, pulling out men we'd already rounded up. I think he got most of his men away with the commander's permission. Good luck to him, in some places he'd have been shot for his trouble. There was a lot of excitement of course but the operation went smoother than some. I felt calm. We were seasoned by now and there were fewer accidents and hardly any panic. Just a few cuts and bruises and a couple of broken legs. We lost only one man, killed by a stray bullet and that his own fault, he was on the wrong side of the ditches. Some civilians made a fuss afterwards and wrote letters and such. They were mostly civil servants, though I heard a few army officers complain that this kind of thing demoralised the regulars. But for the most part it all went without a hitch. Some of us had liquor to drink, it helped harden us when we grew tired. Afterwards the commander lined us up for a speech in which he praised us for bravery and a job well done. Luckily it was a short speech, we were tired and wanting to clean up and sleep it off. Later he got the Knight's Cross, with Swords I think, the same I was promised a year later in Galicia though I never got it. We can't do much with promises.

What the professor said

Remember that it was Heine who wrote *wherever they burn books, sooner or later they will also burn human beings*. Remember that at the very centre of Buchenwald the SS preserved the oak planted in Goethe's memory. This situation is not without its ironies. Remember that they got their power legally, that the body of German law remains intact; it is the simple phrase *protective custody* that puts the Gestapo above law, puts law aside. They are not interested in law and therefore we cannot protest that such and such an action is illegal. Such a comment is irrelevant at this time. It is not merely the lower classes who have been swept up in Hitler's frenzy; though the petty bourgeois has seized power – or its illusion – and though everywhere one sees their tastelessness manifested, though those with power of life and death over millions are for the most part men who have already failed in their former more humble roles as chicken farmers, champagne salesmen, door to door pedlars, cashiered junior officers – though all this is so, it is we of the intelligentsia who have failed, and our failure is the most crucial. I do not mean here to fall into Brecht's attitude; it belittles their crimes to call these men gangsters, to call even their crimes *crimes*; it makes them too familiar, too acceptable. And yet to call them more, to stress their monstrousness, is to deliberately seek a language that can accept them. To do this is, perversely, to ennoble them; the infamous are also famous, history mellows them with its heroics and its victories and even its defeats. A language does not exist in which we can safely discuss them, that does not also taint us. So we must seek a language in which to describe the indescribable and speak of the unspeakable – reaching for this, just as by the same token we recognise the dangers such a language invites, that by its sign we push out the frontier of what becomes acceptable in human conduct. And we are not guiltless, for we have failed most fundamentally in our attempts at objectivity, in our endless questioning without attempting answers. Our order and our language became irrelevant, and in its gaps chaos appeared. So now we have turned over the universities to indoctrination and specious research into racial science. As teachers and as scholars we have ceased to value life, and so we have come to be lifeless, in contempt of the mind and the spirit. Our poets spent themselves contemplating the Apocalypse; small wonder now they should rejoice in its arrival. So we toe the line, we withdraw into silent cynicism; we must admit Streicher as an intellectual yet we no longer mention Heine or Mendelssohn, and in discussing art we have submitted to the dictum that we must confine ourselves to description and not meddle in evaluation. A thousand years of culture have not equipped us for such failure. We stand back wondering who pulled the plug. We are like monks who copy manuscripts in a language no longer understood. In our neglect of feeling, in our long attentions to reason and abstraction and the vaguer emotions, we see now the revenge of emotion. We were beaten too easily; we stood up to reason with them not noticing their contempt for reason is equal to their contempt for law. Too late we realised that, contrary to all our beliefs, man is not rational – or he is not *merely* rational. So here we are with our failures upon us – a cross we must carry through all the stations to the bloody hill. So much for humanism.

I think sometimes of Dürer's painting *The Massacre of the 10,000 Christians*. On every side are the victims, beheaded, stoned, crucified, thrown from the cliff. The butchers are thorough, they gouge out eyes, they kill with mallets and boulders and knives. To the right sits the king on a black horse directing the liquidations. Everywhere the monsters inflict their savagery, whatever occurs to them by way of torture they indulge.

77

There are no rules but that the victims must die. And here is the painter himself, standing in the middle of the work in a world of butchery and terrible suffering. For the moment neither he nor his friend is threatened, and yet their being there is neither mere vanity nor a simple flourish of the painter's brush. Where is the blood? I see none, save a little in the background, and that perhaps provided for the dog to lick: a grace-note of contempt. I see no genitals. I see little expression of agony in the faces of those put to death, or awaiting slaughter; I see neither protest nor resistance. Most of the persecutors seem to care little one way or the other about their work. Was the painter unwilling to get his hands dirty, or should he have messed them up with the blood that was indeed there? The painting was for a patron, the Emperor, in whose feelings for a Moorish atrocity perpetrated on Christians Dürer concurred; the Emperor at this time was trying to raise money for a crusade against the Turks while Luther was advising resistance by the princes against such a tax: the Empire was disintegrating, attempts at unity through foreign campaigns didn't work. Dürer's painting is in a real sense propaganda; for all his admiration of Luther it was from Maximilian that Dürer's pension came. So it's a matter of taste, of what is acceptable to the powerful, that the subject is what it is and that it is without gore. As if in confirmation of this thought I look to the figure of the painter in the painting itself – in the work but apparently not of it. While his face is towards the crucified (two of them and a third cross on the ground awaiting the victim being brought forward wearing again the crown of thorns) – while he is facing that way, his eyes are looking sideways. Perhaps the painter is looking outward at the observer, but I think he is actually looking at the king, the centre of power – the source of wealth and retribution. It is another *Nemesis*. His is the dilemma of the humanist: to perceive suffering, to respond to it, and yet since there's nowhere else for him to turn he turns to the chief assassin to help him speak what he sees. Perhaps it is an accusatory look – and yet it is also covert. He is looking at the source of his own survival whether he looks at the king or at the observer. That source is the origin of misery. The ambivalence on the painter's face arises from the artist's own awareness of his relation with power clouded by his feelings for suffering – his face one way, his eyes another. His companion is Conrad Celtes, the humanist, the writer, a further sign of his dilemma. So he stands there, having executed the work, a man of feeling and intelligence who understands both that he is part of the world he describes and yet apart from it through describing it. There is nothing he can do but stand there uselessly saying *here, I have shown you*, holding up a stick and paper on which he has written his name and date.

Vauru's elm

On the 5th of May 1422 the Bastard of Vauru was dragged through the streets of Meaux and beheaded. His body was taken to be hung on the tree named for him, and his cousin Denis hung beside him. On this tree the Bastard had been accustomed to hang his victims. From the countryside roundabout he would seize working men and drag them to this elm where, if they could not pay ransom, he would hang them. Two years before his death Vauru had taken a young man, he tortured him and demanded ransom. The man sent home to hs wife to gather money from their neighbours. On the given day she came to Vauru and handed over the money, only to find her husband had already been killed. She was like a madwoman then. She was pregnant, she had not long been married, her labour was not far off. They had taken her money and killed her man. For her rage and insolence Vauru had her beaten and hung half-naked on the tree. Night came. Above her hung nearly a hundred corpses, Vauru's victims. The wind rocked the tree, some of their feet brushed against her. And her labour began. Her terrible cries could be heard in the city but no one dared come to her for fear of the Bastard. At length she cried enough to attract the wolves and so, for her, it ended.

Irma

She came from a village in Mecklenburg. In 1933 she was ten years old and eager to join the Bund Deutscher Madchen though her father, strict and respectable, forbade her doing so. She was truly Nordic, blonde and blue-eyed, a good looking woman. Apparently as a child she lacked courage and ran away from fights. She worked first as a trainee nurse, then as a dairymaid. At eighteen she joined the SS. She was drafted for training at Ravensbruck. On her first leave she quarrelled with her father over her membership in the SS and did not return home again. At Ravensbruck Irma, still shy and unaggressive, learned how to beat the women in her charge. She learned how to swallow whatever feelings she may have had in the matter. She was not a sadist. After eight months she was transferred to Auschwitz. She was, says one prisoner, beautiful, so much so that her brutality was unexpected. Irma would appear, elegantly dressed and her hair immaculately set, advancing on the assembled prisoners with her hips swinging. She smiled at the blood she drew and the cries she elicited. She had a whip made for herself from cellophane in one of the camp workshops. She always carried it and used it frequently, even after the Kommandant, Kramer, had forbidden it. She would beat prisoners senseless with this whip or with a walking stick she also carried. In June 1944 she had 350 women locked in a washroom for three days without food, drink, sanitation, or any place to sleep but the floor. She had a prisoner dressmaker, a well-known couturier from Vienna. In need of an abortion, she had a prisoner doctor perform it. She said she wanted to become a film actress. Amongst her lovers, says rumour, were Kramer and Mengele. At the age of 21 she went on trial as a war criminal. She said, in answer to a question, *it might have been that I was frightened as a child, but I grew up in the meantime.* She wept when her sister gave evidence, yet the night before her execution she sang with the other women who were to die with her. She was hanged on the 12th of December 1945.

The last war

After the regular army battles, the destruction of the towns and cities and the burning of the countryside, after the veterans had all been recalled to service, the old men and young men and children and women had all been enlisted and on each side had fought to a standstill, then the cripples were sent for. The combatants' technology now turned to equipping them for battle: limbless regiments, blind squadrons, platoons on crutches manoeuvring to encircle each other. Tanks were built a single finger could operate, airplanes to be flown and devastate by a pilot using only the movements of his teeth and tongue. Artillery, adapted to the control of a foot or a crooked knee, continued shelling even after the last truce had been declared.

I awoke in a ditch as the rockets settled gently to earth, like paper planes. The world was rebuilding itself, the grasses gave off the smell of anaesthetic. Banks of pipes ran everywhere – red, blue, green –

angled over the landscape for mile after mile. Putting my ear to them I could hear a slow steady humming as of plasma or blood being pumped from one continent to another. The land was a battered metal cross, all Europe a spent bullet. In the fine white ash I knelt down, dreaming of my childhood.

The man in the street speaks up for himself

Of course there wasn't much we could do, and we were fed up with things the way they were. I was in the Red Front at first, then I switched to the SA. Also I was in the party, but I wasn't very active in either. Later you had to be in the party to get anywhere, and anyway you couldn't be in the SA and not join. Of course I didn't believe everything, but a lot of it made sense at the time. And then he got into power. Things changed then. Oh, people stopped criticising everything and there was more work and you heard more and more about war as the years passed. We knew it was coming and we'd have to fight for it. People disappeared and some came back. You knew from their silence they'd learned one thing: to keep their traps shut. But we were still giving him a chance to sort things out and it was better than the years and years of nothing. The Jews started going too – you never knew where, but you could work it out. They weren't going to nursing homes. And anyway what of it we said, they were eating us up, that's what we believed then anyway. They'd been grabbing everything and spoiling our women and planting their bastards everywhere, it was only a matter of time. So we struck first. How did I feel about it? Well, it says in their Talmud: *If a man comes to kill you, kill him first.*

But I didn't have much to do with it. I went to meetings and rallies. When the Reichstag went up I went out after Commies, we were furious. On the Night of the Long Knives I kept out of the way, and on the Night of Crystal Glass I pinched a radio and some silverware and broke a few windows. I printed off a few posters for Goebbels' office and helped put them up. Odd jobs. When the typewriters had to be changed I was the one sent round to put in the extra key with the runes. I had a small workshop and made swastika buttons, I was a shopkeeper selling flags and armbands and papers. I took round the collecting box for contributions, I poured petrol on a few books. I ripped medals from the chests of disgraced veterans, I answered the telephone in the Prinz

81

Albrecht Strasse. I was a tailor making uniforms and a cobbler who made jackboots, I sold gold braid to the navy. I was a Blockleiter and compiled dossiers. I drove trucks of Zyklon and dealt in barbed wire on the side. I was a man who could find things, I knew where to get real coffee and wheat flour. Each year I renewed my oath of allegiance. I was a foreman in a factory directing labour brought from the east. I bought up the violins of dead Gypsies, I was curator of the collection of polished skulls of Russian commissars brought to Strasbourg. I was a draftsman, I drew the diagrams for Topf's crematoria patent and in 1952 I drew them again for the new patent. I stamped the J's in the passports, I struck out the names of the Jewish graduates, I helped clear the streets of bums and whores before the Olympics. I was a welder who fixed the exhausts leading back into the vans. I was a labourer, Heydrich hired me to get rid of his mother's gravestone. I drew up timetables, I drove freight trains of deportees to unlonely terminals in the forests. I typed a master's thesis in racial science. Through it all I remembered I had held up a spade at Nuremberg, calling out *I am from Saxony, I am from Bavaria, I am from Prussia*. I dreamed of a farm in the east and thought I would like to settle in the Crimea, I would have plum trees and a grape arbour and a milk cow. I was an air raid warden, I helped dig out dead and living. Every night I had nightmares about the Russians. I was a file clerk paid to keep records and later paid to lose them and then later paid to find them again. I sold my corporal's uniform to an SS general, I drilled boys to fight in the last days, and I fled west and when the Americans came I stood by the roadside begging a cigarette. And I demoted myself to private, and then I was out of work again and broke and hungry as before and for a little while in a prison camp. Then I was released and found work again, and since then I've been doing what I'm doing now and there's no more I can tell.

Simplicissimus's dream

Around me the trees changed, and I saw that in place of leaves were soldiers of all kinds forever climbing and falling, some of them on the lower branches dropping to the ground where they lay dead and useless. Those who were not soldiers formed the roots of the trees, peasants and labourers and skilled tradesmen who as they worked to sustain those above them and to provide for their needs constantly groaned at the labour and the great weight that lay on them. The inert weight of the trees pressed out money from their pockets, cries from their mouths, tears, blood, even the marrow from their bones. All those who could not provide enough for their masters were beaten.

Those higher in the trees were divided by a section that had no branches, a smooth place made slippery so that few could climb it. Those below were troopers and mercenaries, robbers and functionaries who stole from the roots whatever they could for themselves while supplying those above them. Those in the higher parts of the trees bore flags and titles and seals of office entitling them to demand more from those below them, who in turn demanded more from the roots. The highest in rank sat highest in the trees and so on up to the top, where the birds of fortune flew over them showering down gold. Naturally those at the top grabbed most, those at the roots were lucky to get anything at all, and that immediately demanded of them. And all the time those on the trees constantly swarmed about up and down and side to side as chance and the pushing of others determined. Each tree in the forest was so burdened by this arrangement of the population, and as those on the trees skittered about they rocked the trees so that they smashed against each other and many fell off with broken bones and broken heads. *And as I looked I thought all trees were one tree, and sitting at the top of it the war-god, and as this tree covered all Europe with its branches, so it seemed to me it might cover the whole world.*

Reinhard

Patience, Reinhard, patience. What matters is the will and the drive towards power, however devious. Otherwise there's tactics, which is why these files exist, which is why I have grown this infinite patience within myself, like a fingernail, like a long finger of steel. For one day I shall win and it will be all mine, it won't matter then what those other schemers have on me. There is only one way: absolute ruthlessness. What matters is power, and to that end, my patience and my skills.

I have nourished hatred. It too is something you can grow. Whatever blood fights in me I still look right. It's from me the future springs. That stuff we call the masses, they will be cleansed, all those whimperers, pigs calling themselves the people. Only stupidity exists there. They are to be moulded, that only, and I shall mould them. My blood will go singing through them. They will be steel as I am steel, iron as I am, a white metallic fire whose heat I will control.

And I'm devious, cunning enough to do it. Half-drunk, I imagine the bullets I fired into the mirror were my own reflection shooting at me, that it was I who shattered. I shall corrupt from below. I shall send painters into the academies to corrupt the artists, my own priests into the seminaries to bring down the churches from within. I shall have agents out quietly spreading the new language, I shall place my own poets in the salons. The apple will be eaten away from the inside. I would like to build my own camp; the guards would be vicious but it would be called *Camp Fun*. It would be by the sea, on a beach. The guards would wear the masks of idiots, bells and jugglers' caps, they would be dressed as harlequins and circus clowns with great flat feet and the nose and paint and sad looks of Koko. The commandant would be dressed as a Magus and would be addressed by that name. In their fixed smiles the clowns would play tricks, they would beat down the prisoners with happiness or misery painted on their faces. They would throw buckets of water and custard pies, beating with paper clubs and balloons and then with whips. Sometimes the buckets would contain not water but acid. There would always be gay music playing. The guards would supervise backbreaking labour to build vast sandcastles and mud fortifications that would fall down as they were built, and after work the prisoners would enjoy themselves on carousels and swingboats wearing paper crowns and bunting. We would addict them to alcohol and heroin and then deprive them of it. We would kill with merciless laughter.

All the scribblers, seeking order, I'll give them what counts. Grammar, logic, mathematics, law, rhetoric: the fabrications of Europe, the lunatic discoursing eloquently on his lunacy. Lies. Mere conveniences. The madhouse stands on pillars of reason, both jail and asylum. Above, the inmates labour to build and strengthen the pillars; below the pillars drop steadily into the sand. Think of Venice, all its gilded misery sinking into the Adriatic.

At the end I will admit everything. Like Christ, everyone's sin will be mine when they've paid for it in suffering. You want to know who farted downwind? It was me. I snapped off the de Milo's arms. It was I butchered the light from its source: I left the dead with darkness steaming in their mouths. I tattooed the map of my country, hills and rivers and mountains, on the back of a horse and flayed it. I showed no mercy. The man who merely shores up ruins comes to no good: I shall bring things to fullness and wreck them there. I shall claim everything; the great works of death will be named for me. It will be I burned the books and broke every pane of glass on this continent and ploughed through the geometry of Versailles. I committed fellatio and acupuncture on the doorknobs. I abolished the letters M and N, defying everyone to try saying again *murder, man, communism*. I did it all and glimpsed the bits of myself scattered among the thousand fragments of the mirror. It was always flawed, but I shattered it. I kicked in the Mona Lisa smile. I left the iron horse dead and smoking.

But I'm sitting in the bar here alone relaxing with my notions. What I care for is power. The world is a beast to be mastered and broken. It is a horse, I am its rider.

The town

It is difficult to find, a town like many others, a name on the plain. It is a place the borders have shifted many times. People who come from this town argue with each other about their country; each of them thinks of himself as of a different nation. Often it is a matter of the month and year of birth, between the several wars and annexations of territory, always a new flag flying over the town hall. Often it is more complex. *I am Polish*, a man says, *though I was born Austrian. My neighbours call me Russian, my family White Russian. For a while I was Ukrainian. Sometimes I remember that I am Jewish.* The town is small. The road twists out of the forest, for a little while it is the town's main street. Then it is the way through the forest again, the road you must take over the marshes and beyond them the mountains at a great distance. The wooden houses are built more for winter than for summer, the land is poor. On the narrow streets live shoemakers, tailors, chimney sweeps, carpenters, labourers. In the market place there is a large clock with a bullet hole through the ninth hour. When the farmers come into town they sell their goods till sunset, then they buy what they need, gossip, visit acquaintances, perhaps to drink a little wine. At nine they say *it is time to go*, and they leave with their carts and baskets. The town is quiet: someone singing, someone dragging a log, a dog's bark or a distant cry from the river, in a far street an instrument struggling into melody, a woman's scolding.

There is one strange thing: in recent years all the children born here bear each of them a number on one arm. Not printed, it is part of the flesh, a number they bring with them from the womb. Always a different number, sometimes a very high one, but a number that does not wear off, that no scouring will wash away.

One of our objects is missing

Pencil, fibre-tip, spiral notebook, old envelopes covered in scribble, stapler, box of wrong-sized staples, ruler, carbons, Tipp-Ex, two 500 sheet boxes of 210 x 297 mm. (8¼″ x 11¾″) white 71g/m² A4 paper. Workbench made from a door, chair rescued from the bakery skip, picture postcards of the sea. Shelves, stones, bottle filled with alphabet rice, chess pieces, clay egg for a broody hen, the *Obras Completas* of Federico García Lorca in bi-lingual Spanish and Russian, cruciform sea-cat shells, souvenir Budweiser can never opened, collection of foreign stamps, miscellaneous printers' blocks, American Heritage dictionary, five cent lunch tokens, my diary and my world famous collection of unanswered letters. And, as they say, *my battered old Adler*, several keys slithering out of alignment, so many tongues shifting about in the mouth of a drunk unable to say exactly what he means, but saying it anyway, unwittingly, in Freudian slips and typos introduced by the typewriter and the typesetter (*hello again, you*), and by chance. Two rolls of undeveloped film. My glasses, which I have set aside for the moment.

Everything seems to be here: the lighter fuel and the blackened toothbrush for cleaning the keys, even a cup of hot coffee. There's a Cutty Sark whisky bottle on the top shelf, long empty, long kept for the green of its glass where the sunlight strikes here as I work. There are several empty Cornish Wrecks matchboxes, there's a lump of lava and various stones, souvenirs of sundry distant places, several weeds gathered from the banks of rivers, some jars filled with discarded toys set aside by my children as they grew out of them, others with bits of clock parts and baby-eye shells. Oddments of no use, a shop or a bank of images. Sheep bones from Dartmoor, whitened and faintly green in the long rain.

But there's something I can't put my finger on. Something I can't find, that is not here. I cannot even think what it is. I have no image of it, only a sense of its being missing, gone away, gone astray. Not here.

Pocketed, perhaps, by some guest of the house, one like myself, an aficionado of interesting objects, souvenirs, *items*. Or carried off by the cat, borrowed but not put back by someone I live with, dropped along the way. But by whom? And then more questions, hunts, interrogations.

Better to let it go. Objects have lives of their own, and are sometimes with us, sometimes visiting, sometimes gone forever. Books and hats are the same. I have a library through which books move; some vanish forever to be replaced by books I've never seen and would not otherwise have read. Animals live this way, cats and dogs that stay awhile and move on.

But still the feeling: something missing.

Something has fallen off from my life at some point I wasn't looking, when my attention was elsewhere no doubt. Whatever it was, whatever it still is somewhere, it took itself off into the shrubbery that fans out from the edge of what little I know and thickens darkly into absolute ignorance.

Our children are like this. Sometimes I imagine I can hear them growing, preparing for a long road ahead without us. Like objects, they have their own autonomies.

And still it bothers me, this missing object. I would be content to know what it was, and remember what it had to do with me for a while, and let it go. I keep reminding myself, banging myself on the forehead till it's flat and I'm punchdrunk, *everything has to be let go*. We own nothing and no one. 'It's not like me to hang on to anyone' a woman I loved said once, at long last. I keep her picture in a secret place.

And what else? My watch, my clothes, my books, driftwood, notes for *the book of distances* I've yet to write, messages from some I knew. All here. Dust, water hissing in the pipes, record player singing in some other room of the house, and outside the street, garden, traffic, footsteps, things to do and be done out there in the world, the garden to be dug over for winter, the front door to be painted blue now my eldest daughter is sixteen. The Amish, who live quietly along the borders of states for rapid getaway, paint their doors blue when they judge their daughters eligible and young men may come a-calling in their pony carts and their beardless credentials.

But what is it that is missing here? Or why do I catch at the sense of something missing? Why do I feel it, nagging away like a pain in an amputated leg, like a telephone in a locked room, like a distant burglar alarm in the rainy night? Why does it give cause to such rhetoric?

I must have had a use for it, if only in companionship.

I prepare to write a sonnet. I have work to do, I am not concerned with minimalism, and can't be doing with fuss. This is the twentieth century, I have a living to earn, a mortgage, a wife and children to support, or go through the motions of supporting. I live in the West Country or in Barnsley, where I have a real existence all my own. And so I prepare to write a sonnet. I get the bowls out, and the measuring cup and the scales, the cutting board, sharp knife, blender, matches for the stove.

90

I assemble the ingredients: floury white bags of sturdy adjectives, jars of assorted nouns, a couple of pints of verbs. Plenty of prepositions, assorted gerunds, any amount of articles, various lengths of clauses in apposition and miscellaneous adjectival clusters for decoration.

But I'm out of adverbs. In the supermarket I meet my daughter. She is buying solid useful things: fruit, cheese, toothpaste, tights, for a journey she is to make tomorrow. I select my adverbs, and we share a trolley. We pass a slowly moving middle aged couple, he pushing their cart, she taking jars and tins from the shelves, checking their prices, examining labels and weights and tables of contents. She is about to put a small jar of cherries into the trolley when her husband says *You're deviating from the list again, dear.* She puts her cherries back, and looks to the torn envelope of her shopping list. My daughter catches my eye and giggles. I giggle. We take a sudden deep interest in Chicken Chow Mein packaging. My daughter begins picking up and putting down Portuguese sardines. We leave the supermarket and go home. I go back to my Adler, and my waiting sonnet.

The world is not ordered. Or rather: the orders imposed on the world are merely convenient or coincidental and have nothing to do with it. The world is other. I can't make much sense of it. I concur with common sense, but that is merely like agreeing to speak in a certain language, for the time being, on some matter or other, or using trigonometry to solve a particular problem. I find the world without order, or at any rate without ours.

The phone rings. *Sheila* says a strange woman's voice. *Sheila with the fat face. Is this the electric? How much for rock and roll?* I put the phone down. I don't know anything about this, honest Guv. The phone rings again. *How many trees do you want?* says a brisk man's voice, and the phone goes dead.

I sit down to write a list of names. They are the names of real people: Mr Purse my bank manager, Mr Carver my dentist, Messrs Slugget and Pow both butchers, Mrs Trim who is a dog beautician in Bridport, and Mr Tripp who is the mace-bearer at the University. But if I wrote them down, as characters in a fiction, everyone would think I'd made them up.

I'm mystified, and so might you be, gentle reader. You do right to ask 'What does all this have to do with the sturdy citizens of Budleigh Salterton?' I'm mystified by strange Japanese students arguing Kant and Hegel in loud voices in the Duke's Bar of the Clarence Hotel, by stray comments in the street and supermarket, voices in the parlour saying very firmly *no I won't go away till he sees me.*

And by this problem of some thing that's missing. I hadn't forgotten about that. I guess the tingling is normal, and the sense of bored mystification. And the vertigo.

I make lists of my faults: fits of self-consciousness, a fascination with all things grotesque, a mind that slithers about and won't stay on anything but is easily distracted by a random question such as *are willow trees deciduous?*, and then is concentrating its grainy eye on the willows along the river. And mild fits of hypochondria, my kleptomania, my laziness, sloppiness, bouts of bad temper.

And something else. A thing that if it were here would immediately demonstrate its reason for having gone.

Or something I used to be rather than something I used to have.

But it ain't heah, Mistuh Buggooh. It jess ain't heah no mowa.

I shall have to go back. I shall have to go back over my life again, slowly, like a nun counting her beads, a child his marbles, a miser his coins, a shrew her orgasms.

I shall have to examine it all from the outside. I shall have to invent someone else to be me and watch him closely, rerunning the film frame by frame till I find the place where whatever went absent without leave from my life went away. Only then will I know whether I want the damned thing back.

I invent another name for myself, another identity, another biography. Everyone else and everything else is the same and in place, as before, but I am Jack now. My name is Jack.

His name is Jack.

Jack gets up from his desk, irritated with his lists, with his day wasted away again with trivia. He goes downstairs and makes a pot of tea. His younger children come in from school, his wife comes home from work, they eat supper, exchanging details of their day's events. Jack has nothing much to report. He's been to the supermarket, answered the telephone, made a shepherd's pie, and he's been thinking. *Thinking again* she says. *You'll give yourself a headache.*

After supper they go out, noticing as they do all the clocks have stopped, each one keeping a perfect record of where it got to in time. They take a bus into the city, he trying to remember a tune, distracted when she speaks, the tune almost in his head, almost in his larynx. He almost has it. It vanishes.

In the cathedral. *Why* she says, and he readily agrees, *this is not a cathedral at all. It's a huge museum of baking.* They walk about in it, examining great decorated cakes in stone and wood, some hanging from the ceilings like upturned tables of feasts these warriors may have had. They stare up into the icy flutings. There are pastry shapes of people, great painted cakes of fallen lordlings with their ladies side by side, some stacked above their children, one with her feet resting on the piped necks of two swans, the work of some medieval master baker. *Not stone*, she says, *but pastry. And marvellously done.* One great crusty pie is called, in the language of the other world, a pulpit, another the bishop's throne. Others are pastry moulds, cut outs, gingerbread men disguised as ancient saints, the dead in the open boats of their shrouds. Some are hacked at by the levellers, or by Cromwell's lot, who didn't care for such fancy workmanship. And there are friezes moulded in marzipan, piped and finely chiselled across the nave. Above, the fancy work increases. Below lies the plainer fare of townsfolk, merchants and benefactors who could not get into heaven on richer food than the plain loaf tablets remembering their names. *Best I like here* she says, *Sir John Speke who never says a word.* They stand by the effigy of a young man, a great hunk of brown bread, and pay him their respects. His legs are uncrossed, signifying he did not die in battle. He is young, long haired, handsome, a tragic death no doubt. Around him on the walls and ceiling his cakes are fluted and stamped with his initials, his animals the two headed eagle and the hedgehog. Or is it a wild boar, a porcupine, or some sort of armadillo? *Or maybe*, she suggests, *a totem animal. A totem animal that no longer exists or never existed.*

That's it he thinks. *That's it. That's what's missing. That's what I don't have. Or never had. Or lost. A totem animal.*

They stare up at the hanging cakes, the vulvae of anemones among the sea's rocks.

They leave the cathedral, still talking about cakes and bread and pastry, he thinking about his totem animal. She takes his arm, he is still thinking about the totem. He looks at her. She's still with him, then, old 38B cup.

He's still with her. He thinks he's almost figured out what's missing. It's her, on every third consonant, every tenth heartbeat, every other thought. She's only intermittent, their marriage is growing faint, he thinks suddenly for the first time and defines her in his mind as *my first wife*. He has a sense of there being six gears to this marrying business but they've only ever found forward and reverse together. He pushes it all back to the back of his mind, and thinks some more about his missing animal.

And there we leave them. There we leave him, Jack out with my wife, wondering what to do next and where to go and what is it in him gives him this feeling of something missing. They meet Charley and Charley's wife. They enter a local hostelry, and in the debased language of their time ask for what is in these regions loosely referred to as *beer* which they pay for in the debased currency they have about themselves. Jack remembers the tune he couldn't remember, the theme from *Casablanca*, and sings it. They drink more beer, and gradually he forgets that anything at all is missing, and if he thought about it any more would no doubt conclude nothing was. They have a terrific night out in town. They always do.

Goodbye Jack, out with my first wife.

Goodbye Jack.

The history of stones

Only a stone, he said. A small one. All the same she wanted it moved, it did not belong on her mantelpiece. His stone, her mantelpiece, he noted. He spread his hands, indicating other things they gathered: dried grasses, feathers, wheels, old clock parts, teazels, thistles, honesty leaves, lumps of ant-blazoned bark from felled elms, branches water had turned to artefacts. So why not stones? It seemed she objected to stones, to their presences, their lumpiness, their bulk. They were not pretty, like flowers. They were not feminine. In vain he argued that stones were genderless, that their likenesses to bird or breast or fist or penis were human notions, after the fact, nothing to do with their being stone. *Stone.* She glared at him across her shoulder. Their house was too small for stones, she said. And there were children now. He shrugged. It was only a stone. One stone. It marked the beginning of his obsession: the stone that sometimes she removed and sometimes he replaced on the shelf beside the shell and the chipped porcelain shepherdess. Its movements marked their movements. It was the first of other stones accumulating in corners, drawers, cupboards, boxes, in little piles around the house.

Visiting some ancient hill fort, half its three defensive rings cut off centuries ago for corn land, he looked across the waving wheat at half a county and three river valleys to the sea, far off, and northward to the higher hills towards the other sea. Other hill positions aligned with this one, watching for the coming of armed strangers. Seeking some memento of the place's farmers and warriors and their women, dogs and scruffy children, he broke one slab of sandstone on another to snap away a piece he carried with him to stand end up on his workshop table. A wedge, shaped into a fist some four inches high, two shades of brown either side of a vertical strip of quartz, trapezoid. A stone fitting the grip well, not a weapon but a weapon's emblem. Like a helmet, or a blunted spear.

They walked across the hill, a Sunday outing, taking paths that were the ancient ways into the city. Years ago they had discovered the hill, its sudden opening out on top across a gate between the hedges where was further hill, village, road, smoke, orchard, sheep, green of adjoining parishes. She pointed out the pattern of the sower's quick machinery across the opposite slope that later, now, appeared as his signature scribbled amongst the sprouting wheat. They discussed the landscape, verifying its effects on each other: crow and copse and farm chopped up by motorway. And hills that seemed running after each other into darker greens, red clay showing where the ploughs had cut, and beyond on the topmost line where the Atlantic winds struck unhindered between the green land and the long blue, a dutch barn, empty, distant, sliver of a fingernail. Or did they walk across the hill only or did they walk on to the village for tea and cakes, and why not both they disagreed, passing on the narrow path beside the iron gate a girl with a dog staring into the hedge. She stopped them. *Look at the gatekeeper* she said, and they looked at the butterfly she'd seen in the briars. *They're rare now* she told them. *And growing rarer.*

As some men collect stamps or matchboxes or train numbers, he collected stones. At first a general collection, a heap, a random scattering of stones he picked up here and there as they struck his attention. Stones that were souvenirs, remembrances of places and particular events. Some that were unique, chosen for their shapes, their colours, shadings, coldness, soothing in his palm. Others that were more particular in shape and formed departments of his collection: a few rare items, perfectly round, a few others that were egg shaped, some that were hollowed out into boxes by weather, one or two like coins, one like a latchkey. Two that matched each other, that were chalk figurines holed through and seamed by tides and burrowing creatures into limbs and body and head, perfect mother shapes. Breasts. Knuckles. Bellies. Shoe shapes.

Junk, she said. *Litter. Clutter. Useless.* Hoping that as the children grew and they moved to a larger house he would not pack and move them. He did.

His work was to make precise life-size replicas of common domestic objects: a sponge, a spoon, a garden fork, matchboxes, a typewriter, a gin bottle, a jar of mustard. They were used for demonstration purposes. It served him well enough for employment. For diversion he found other things to do. He would enter a department store and steal say a tube of toothpaste. In his room he would carefully unpick the tube's seal, remove the cap, and blow out all the paste. Resealing the tube carefully so that it looked full yet was empty he put it back into its box and replaced it on its counter in the store. These were his secret jokes. He would never be there to hear the punchlines nor learn their outcomes, and he never told anyone about them so as to prolong the diversions, turning them in his memory, adding details that had never happened. One day, bored with his job of making replicas, he drove past his place of work saying *dammit no* and drove on to the beach. There he collected in the boot of his car some forty beach stones, round or flat or otherwise, and having wandered about all day thinking of his life and its ramifications staring at gulls and seagrass and tankers in the baymouth, drove home. That evening he took the stones to his workshop and there made hollow copies of them in fibreglass, and the next day returned with the stones and their doubles to the same beach where in the tide the fake stones bobbed and drifted several days, and there were reports made to the press of stones that floated in those parts.

Time passed. He went back to work, making replicas, the only trade he knew, and with the mortgage and the family to think of, he went back to it. It wasn't her fault he was tied, though he hoped at first it might be, she was convenient to his sulky humours when he cursed the days of sameness. For her part she made her own copies from the pattern books and recipes provided, produced a typed original with carbons and then as many xeroxed copies as were needed of the several contracts made between them both on the one hand and between them and the rest of the planet on the other. He settled to his work, grew more detached from it, and then more skilled in it. His replicas became exemplars, used for exhibition purposes, he was sent for from other places to demonstrate his craft, he became a journeyman to his trade and travelled to distant centres, lecturing, teaching, showing slides and examples of his products, demonstrating their manufacture, paid to show others how to make copies of the copies he made. His life became more tolerable, more varied, more interesting, and slightly more affluent. Their house grew more exotic with the things brought from distant parts, though as often as not what he fetched from foreign continents was a stone or two amongst the presents for her and the children. She was pleased with his success. She encouraged him in everything but the stones. Sometimes she travelled with him, and took the opportunity to throw them out of the suitcases before returning. He went on collecting them: each place he went he picked a stone, usually from the sea-smoothed pebbles of the world's beaches. He liked to think of himself carrying them from one place to another, digging into his pocket on some far shore for a stone he'd picked from some other distant littoral, and swap it there, replacing it with another that he would carry some place he'd not yet been.

She dug her heels in, collecting in his absence all the stones piled everywhere about the house. She'd work to do herself, she said, without coming home to a house full of stones that gathered cat fur and dog dust and children's sticky sweet wrappers. Could he not at least keep them in a shed in the garden, or confine them to his own room and would he stop altogether for God's sake, please, collecting them? His clothes were baggy from transporting them. His pockets bulged and tore with them. He was like a pack camel. He began to find it necessary to hide them from her, depositing them in secret places amongst his shirts and tools. She still found them, and removed them to the porch, from where they'd wander back into the house, again appearing amongst the furniture and ornaments.

Stones made from other stones, composites, conglomerates, stones made from ancient sands cemented together and in the rise and fall of oceans and the movements of earth shaped to fit his hand. Basalt of feldspar and augite, dark lava, brecchia, chert, flint, gabbro, karst and marlstone, pudding stone, gneiss and grit and granopyre and granite, shales, sandstones, slates, oolite and other limestones, gravels, tufa and tuff and quartz, stones veined with minerals, igneous, sedimentary, calcarous, plutonic, carbonaceous. He gathered them for complexity and for simplicity: colour, shape, interlayering of surfaces and shades: a scrap of white lias from Lyme Regis, a fishfin embedded in it; jet rock and black marl from the lower Jurassic; Portland Stone; Purbeck marble. And a bit of soft brick, tipped over a cliff and sea-worked into a soft red pebble. Another that was a red-black sliver of stone, an arrowhead he smoothed between the crook of his forefinger and thumb the many miles he covered. They were all his stones.

From Cape Cod he picked a piece of what seemed to be lava, and from Lake Wachusett a lump of Indian paint stone, red where the oxide dabbed his wetted finger. From Lake Michigan he took a small lump of stone and rusty iron and nails framed round the half buried brass wheel of an old Meccano set, part perhaps of the debris of the Chicago fire tipped in the lake and oozed over to the Wisconsin shore. A flat stone from the same place he dropped in California, and from there a bit of reddish stone he buried in woods near Kansas City, in the middle of that continent. From Long Island he selected a white round stone that he brought with a similar piece from Quebec and with these two established some relation between the Sound and the St Lawrence and the beach at Budleigh Salterton in Devon, from where he was unable to choose a stone at all, they were so many and smoothly shaped and iridescent in the tide mark he gave up trying, and took none. From the northern shores of Caithness he took a piece of granite he exchanged with a similar piece at Land's End. He sent a stone ahead of himself to Africa, collected it when he arrived in Nairobi, carried it to Lagos, brought it home again, and picked a name at random from the New Delhi telephone book, and mailed it anonymously and without explanation to that address. He twinned beaches in Brittany with beaches in Spain by exchange of stones. He took a bit of grit from Stonehenge and when in Australia at Ayers Rock chucked it at the rock, and picked a sliver of its stone he years later deposited at Gay Head, on Martha's Vineyard. It was his secret work. He discussed it with no one.

Stones with the shapes of bear, of fish, of bird's wing. Blue/green flinty stones from Point of Ayr on the Isle of Man, and from the beach at Peel a blue stone marked with white like the oars of a boat, perhaps of the Vikings who built the castle there. White soft chalk pebbles from the North Sea shore, with holes bored through by whirling sand grains, that he found were called dobie stones and used to repel evil. He placed them above his door, hung them on strings, weighted the end of the bathroom pullswitch with one of them. Others were doorstops, paper weights, icons that when dropped again in water glittered their many shaded brilliances. Stones shaped in all weathers, scraped beneath glaciers, ground by the sea on other stones, some like fruit, some like weapons, a stone from Vermont like a black knife blade, and a green stone with greener markings from the southern coast that seemed the brushwork of a mandarin calligrapher.

And the letter stones: one for his daughter, a blue and yellow lime-stone imprinted white in the lines of quartz spelling her initial; a flat stone where the cracks spelt clearly an E in the green; a stone in which tiny barnacles had built an S against the blue; stones bearing K's, N's, O's, F's, H's, L's, T's, an X or so. And a stone in the shape of the letter C he gave to his wife. Her stone. But she was not to be suckered, and let it lie. He arranged and rearranged them, his stoney scrabble set, planning to complete the alphabet, wondering whether some message could be read from them, and if so what it would say.

He grows older, he approaches the middle of his life, he falls subject to vague aches and sharper moments of terror, he lies awake with his insomnia hearing the blood in his temples thump the pillow, he grows more easily short of breath, he takes more exercise, it does him less good, he curses the travelling and the work he does though others envy his mobility, he forgets names and significant details, his wife complains he neglects her and the children, he retreats more and more into his own skull where he feels walled up, his children grow unbidden, he feels the press of other generations close behind, he thinks he has done little and believes such success he's had to be both illusory and ephemeral, his wife grows bored with it all and takes a lover, he begins to suspect it, he grows convinced of his own failure wondering what else to do, he fears death and age, resents the coming failings of his body, his wavering sexual potency, finds much that's thought art mere entertainment and distraction and propaganda, he crosses out the names of his friends as they die from his address book, he stares blankly into open space for long periods of time, he misses his wife in her more frequent absences, he blames himself for them, he collects more stones.

By Lake Champlain I walked, far off, a long day amusing myself among the weekenders, kids rowing, motorboats, stately pleasure craft, swimmers, skin-divers, water-skiers, picnickers, the folk with summer houses along the shoreline playing cards and drinking out the hot September Sunday. In my pocket I carried three stones, one you gave me love that's round and small as you are and carries in its centre what you say's a kiss, another I picked up by Walden Pond amongst the beercans just below the passing Boston transit trains by Thoreau's vanished cabin in the woods, the third a stone given me by a friend now dead who brought it from Mount Etna. I considered which to leave amongst the dark shales of the beach, could part with none of them, and added to these three a black sliver that's brother to the marble of those parts.

In time he foresaw it: stones piled in every part of the house, in baskets and on specially constructed racks, no room for anything. Surely she'd succeed in drawing a limit to the number he'd gather. *It's only fair* she said in his imagination somewhere in the cluttered future of their lives where he'd have named and dated and coded with the details of their origins the stones of his collection, set up filing and cross reference systems, begun to move towards a computerised retrieval method. It would form a national collection, a peculiar asset to the community, offered on his death in lieu of taxes to the state. Before that she would hint more strongly that a home was meant for something more than stones, flouncing out, there were too many, some stones were turning up in bed with them. Meanwhile he was writing up the histories of stones, their ancestries of bone and mollusc and water siftings, derivations out of marsh plants, genealogies of magma and violence, earth fold, seas that piled and nagged and abandoned beaches, rivers fanning out out their silts, effects of rain and frost and heat, rocks splitting into pebbles, stones forming other stones. Meanwhile she was losing interest in the losing struggle. Her lover was a man of action. Her lover was dynamic, living in the present, gregarious, outspoken, sociable, ambitious, many-sided, vulnerable. He was not ponderous and stoney like her husband, always peering down into microscopes, checking mineral counts and crystal lattices, fascinated that the stones outlasted him and her and all their squabbles.

He began replacing some of them, keeping them a while, aware his life was how short a time compared with their time. A stone from Mexico he carried twice across the Atlantic, touched the earth with it in Albany New York and Anglesey Wales, touched other stones, and after some three further years its lying in a drawer returned it to the beach he'd taken it from, when again in that country.

Some he gave away, or handed on to others asking that they take the stones on a journey, leaving them some place of their own choosing. Some he deliberately lost, many he buried in the garden. He still collected stones, but chose fewer with more fastidiousness. Now he merely borrowed them. His collection stabilised. He adopted a rule: as he gathered one stone he discarded another .

But it was too late.

He came to realise the best place to keep the stones he picked was in the places where he found them. He began merely to note them, name some, handle one or two, put them down again. He resolved to put them all back, one by one.

Stone fell from the sky. Stone rose in the depths of the earth, part of rock, part of boss and outcrop, part of everything. Stone was tree, stone was windblown dust, stone was river wash and cemented silica. Stone was the deposit of chemical spring or the housing of tiny ocean creatures, stone was their accumulated fallen bones, stone was the body of an animal long extinct. Stone was ancient mud printed with bird's foot. Stone was axehead, scraper, hammer, anvil. Stone was shaped in the hands of masons, carvers, sculptors, slaves laying tesselated pavements for their masters' feet. Stone was Ordovician Trilobite, so much older than the man holding it that his life beside its endurance was the one cry of his mouth opening his last groan anywhere in the long dark. Stone was Spirifer Undiferus in the deep Permian layer, stone was fern printed shale from the coal seams, stone was Ammonite, Hoplites Dentatus from Folkestone. Stone was Actinocamax Plenus from the chalk of the Dover escarpment. Stone was stone.

She would leave him at last. She would pack her suitcase. She would select the things that were hers, divide the twenty years of their intermingled lives and possessions, she would sleep for the last time in this bed with him, and she would leave. He was a stone. His life was becoming stone. Their marriage had become stone. His speech was all stone, his hands cold and dry and stoney with the stones he handled, his body stone, his face stone, his breath stone. She would leave him. It would make little difference to him. He would merely replace the spaces she abandoned with more stones.

Stone of the Bivalve from the Cretaceous, a layer at times 50,000 feet thick and 135 million years old, younger than the Triassic stones in its company, the Silurian, the Cambrian, the first rocks from which these rocks descended. And yet the stones of which this stone was made: all the same age, the same grains, the same molecules, the same atoms that were hot gas blown out of the sun, the hand holding the stone the same age: everything old, the same age as all the entrails of the primal atom, still resonating to the music of the big bang; the entire universe the same. All that's new is my holding it, this blue fossil. And my knowing it.

He remembered the stone the giant squeezed in his fist and forced water from. He looked around for the stone David slung at Goliath, the stones thrown at the woman taken in adultery, the stone Jacob used for a pillow. He picked up stones from the falling castles of the Middle Ages. He sought tiny grains carried in the feet of birds across oceans. He found stones melted in the heat of the first atomic explosions. He touched stones carried as ballast in the holds of eighteenth century Dutch freighters, used later as building stone. He examined the stones used to weight murder victims dumped in the marshes of Jutland. He stood in the drizzle of neutrinos that passed through him and all the stoney planet as if through patches of mist. He touched a stone brought down from the moon.

Travelling, living his life, working his trade with the replicas, he held to other secret purposes. Swapping stones around the beaches of the world he fancied he was confusing future geologies. How, they'd ask a million years hence, did this black tinstone commonly found in Cornwall turn up in Tasmania? No wandering Phoenician boat could account for that, no movements of ice or ocean currents, nor for this northern soapstone found in Egypt and this Scandinavian schist turned up in Tunisia. How else, but fancifully, explain the shaped Labrador flint discovered in a grave in Greenland, brought there in the body of a dying Viking after some encounter with the Esquimaux of Labrador? Explanations there would be, but neither trade nor nature would explain his rearrangements of the beach stones. It was his secret work, confusing in one lifetime as many of the globe's pebbles as possible by shifting them about its surface. At his life's end, he smugly assured himself, things wouldn't be as at his birth on the planet.

But if there were a secret employment in shifting stones, who, he wondered, might be his secret employer? Perhaps he only seemed to employ himself as a journeyman in order to carry out this larger trade in stones, and even his apparent whims as to which stone to select, which discard where, all part of a larger scheme. Later in life he began to think less and less he did it for his own amusement, and there were darker days he saw his habit's pointlessness, and wondered further than his fancy that his compulsion merely screwed up geology. Old fears touched him, sitting in some plane or train: that one journey must be his last, one stone his last trophy plunging with him in the wreck, outlasting by millenia his sight and touch of it. He sat nervous in traffic, soothing the stone in his palm. Age moved in. His children grew and left, came back to tease him, taunted him with images of their mother. He gave them each particular stones to remember him by. They pocketed them. They humoured him. Making love for the last time with his wife he had glimpsed all the men and women of the last few thousand years delighting in each others' flesh, gasping their oblivions. His heart knocked more heavily more often. He chose one particular stone to hold within his hand at death and travel with him into the ground. *Years away*, he assured himself, and threw the stone into the hedgeback, and wondered further what the real nature of his travelling and moving stones might be, and on whose behalf if anyone's did he act?

He grew older, he considered retirement, he gave up smoking. His friends moved or died or found new friends, his children visited less and less, and then sent only their children. He thought less and less of his vanished wife, and missed her less. He grew more irritable, talked less and less to anyone including himself, he gave up sex, he gave up drink, he gave up movies and theatre and chess and music. He played patience and read cheap paperbacks. He travelled less. He ceased collecting stones, and one by one got rid of all the stones he had.

You will recall the stone carrier: by the nature of his work he travels widely, and by nature of diversion he collects exchanges and redistributes small stones around the world. A childish and harmless enough occupation, which he discusses with no one, it raises no questions. He is a familiar figure crossing as he often does the frontiers of nations. The customs and border officials think it nothing strange to find within his baggage lumps of slate and quartz and sand stone. By now they know him well enough. His stones have no commercial value, there are no regulations as to their import or export. The officials are used to him, tapping the sides of their skulls and saying in their several languages here comes the crazy stoneman with his bag of rocks. All this we have foreseen: he is familiar with procedures of this nature. We have arranged then that on his next commission he will carry a particular stone to a destination in South America. It is a stone originally picked up in County Clare. It will be his intention to get rid of it. In South America he will give this stone to a stranger who makes his acquaintance in one country and travels with him to another, who will reveal in conversation a similar interest in stones. In return the stranger will give him a stone, requesting him to drop it on a certain beach on a certain day. The stone will seem innocuous enough, ordinary, boring, banal. But this stone is particular. It is a drug to drive a continent insane, enslave a president, demolish a civilisation, derange a hemisphere. All this we have arranged. It is about to happen.

He shut the paperback novel. He shuddered, dozed, read again, looked through the plane window at the dark Atlantic night, forgot which way he was travelling, into or away from the sun. He shut the paperback: the meeting in the panelled room adjourned, the plotters dispersed, all fingerprints removed, all record of their meeting and its subject – the stone carrier, the stone from County Clare – the secret hidden in the most obvious place: in the million copies of the book he was reading. He accepted uneasily a brief conversation with his neighbour, a man who confessed a habit of carrying stones from place to place. The plane flew on into the blackness, its destination Lima, Peru.

Nothing happened. He resisted all further attempts at conversation by his neighbour, kept the Irish stone in his pocket, refused to examine the grey pebble his travelling companion tried to draw attention to. In Lima he completed his business as soon as possible, met no one, travelled on, accepting no companionship as he flew to Brazil. He gave no stone to anyone, nor accepted none. He flew north to New York, thence to Princeton, visited the sandy beaches of Ocean City, shuttered and wintry, but neither dropped nor collected any stone there.

He kept the stone, made no new acquaintance, spent as little time as possible in Ocean City, cut short his visit to North America, flew home to the one spot on the planet anyone endured his indifference. Arrived, he took the stone from County Clare from his pocket, and placed it on the mantel. It was the last stone left of his collection.

He kept the stone a further month or so and took it on a trip into Yorkshire. At Whitby he wandered down into the harbour: gulls, fishing boats, men gutting cod. He spoke the river's name, *Esk*, and stared at the shaley sandstones of the cliffs known locally as Dogger. In his pocket was his last stone. He would throw it in the harbour.

And what if all this moving of stones around the world were really part of something larger, elements moving in a vector that with the placing of the last stone would discharge what energies? In all this chance and circumstance of all his choice of stones and their placings was perhaps one final result: a flood of energy, a burst of power, one point in time to be reached where in this sector of the creation highest perfect enlightenment comes about at last, all the lights winking out in the sky, and then nirvana. Boom Boom. Perhaps. Perhaps nothing. The gulls as before, the fishermen as before, the trawlers as before. He took the stone from his pocket, and drew his arm back to throw it far out into the harbour, thinking out his little purpose in rearranging stones finally complete, his life as pointless as it ever had been, the vector set, and briefly every stone on earth aligned and the last fitted in the long assembling of a mechanism that released at last its spark of energy into the cosmos. Perhaps.

He pitched the stone far out amongst the gulls and drifting fish guts on the flat water of the harbour. It was evening, the sun gone behind the land, the fishermen's voices sharp but what they said lost among the other sounds. The stone flew from his hand, arching through the still air and the evening. It hit calm water, splashed briefly, a gull dipped to it and decided no, the stone sank. The universe and all its lights flicked off then, for him who threw the stone, for ever.

Not quite Buster Keaton

First frame:

The hills, neither high nor long, bare but for trees right and left at the edges of the frame. At the frame's foot a hedge, lank and untrimmed. In the upper half of the frame blank sky, almost cloudless, high and blue as it ought to be for the month, which is June in a heatwave, the sunlight starkly across like a smear on the lens. Down the middle of the frame a single track roadway of concrete slabs, recently constructed, snakes right then left then right again to the farm, the only road in or out. It forms a large Z through the lower green half of the frame as seen from where we are, and cuts a slight dip at the hill's crest. From there looking back these indications of direction would be reversed, and we'd be visible as small figures wandering about in farm buildings. Where we are is basking in the green of northerly Devon before the landscape toughens towards the coast, in occupation of the old manor-house, where we are running old movies, drinking a lot of cider, and trying to make a film without benefit of cameras. In the meantime, waiting for the projectionist to arrive, we are putting imaginary frames around everything, discovering how much depends on point of view, and what a difficult and troublesome labour is adjusting to Heisenberg's Uncertainty Principle.

So, from our position in time and space, the road comes in down the frame. Cattle graze either side of the road, which is unfenced, and on the left side of the roadway as we see it there's a low bank, in shadow mostly, topped by slight bushes, gorse or fern. At this distance it's not possible to tell.

We walk to the river to smoke and throw stones. The river is low, on account of the drought. *On account of:* now that, surely, someone says, is an Americanism. Or sloppy English. We resist the impulse to wade over to the other bank of the drought struck river, where we'd then be standing as we are staring as we are as if we'd approached the river from the opposite direction. There would be the same water, the same lily pads, the same dragonflies. We look back to the farmhouse, seeming to be above hedges all thatch, like a shepherd's pie, beyond it the hill and the Z of the incoming road, where a white van is turning left and then right. It brings our projectionist.

A cast of thousands approaches the brow of the hill on the hill's other side. They have not yet entered our frame, and we cannot yet see them. What we can see are the cattle on the hilltop, scattering from the van

108

against the skyline.

One in the afternoon, the heat building into haze, a Harrier jumpjet howling fast over the hill a swift moment uses the house as target practice. Whatever we were thinking or waiting for, we're dead. The jet vanishes. Did it happen? We were napalmed and cluster bombed, the ancient barn and manorhouse thatch a blaze of flame. We consider ourselves part of the body count. We have been taken out, and queue at the cider flagon for a while, vaguer and vaguer in the heat.

Second frame:

Soon Mr Laurel and Mr Hardy will be dismounting from the London train and taking the bus to Okehampton, loaded down with Christmas trees and battered runaways' suitcases, ladders and parcels and open buckets of white paint. They'll arrive hot and sweaty and irritable, batting each other with their bowlers, exasperated. *Look what a fine mess you've gotten me into. Won't somebody, please, do something to help me?* And there'll be Minnie and Donald and Mr Magoo. And best of all there'll be Keaton with his hands in his pockets, whistling, the projector over his shoulder and his detective manual in his pocket.

Over dinner the invention of suitable topics, for instance the dining table, which is oak, immense, scored, used, the house surely built round it, a table magnificent and sufficient for God to bear an image of in his mind. And should God forget about tables, surely this one would endure, demanding great thoughts be thought around it, and good dinners.

And then from room to room exploring, looking for ghosts. And in the afternoon returning to the river conversing with the dragonflies: blue, green, sparks of spat metal, bits of volcano, their wings as they settle pulsing like lungs. With his front legs the insect cleans his face, turning the large black bead of his head through impossible angles from side to side. But the head doesn't fall off. The bulging eyes remind us of the unopened eyeballs of the dead bird in the barn. The dragonfly continues his toilet, arcing his long body for cleaning. Straightens out. Pulses. And without visible preparation or obvious movement is suddenly gone.

Back to the garden, the kitchen, the yard, to the falsification of documents.

The falsification of documents:

He's locked himself in to the barn, by mistake. In the huge dark room, cool even in this weather, he sits down to wait. A piano he can't play, a door he can't open. The barn has been blacked out for the film show. It smells richly of creosote. A little light slips in around the blinds, and he concentrates on this, on its reflections on the floor and the piano and the whitewashed walls. On the floor, transfixed by the shaft of sunlight through the fingerhole in the door he can't open, lies a small dead bird, recently hatched, where it has fallen to its hardboard death, its little wings splayed out, featherless and naked and blind.

Keaton points the projector into his mouth. The film flickers over his teeth, illuminating cigarette smoke and the wandering moths of the barn. Across Keaton's tongue Bogart, his body grey with sand and flies, is with great difficulty dragging a boat through tall reeds, sweating and cursing. We note his sardonic grin.

The Oglala Sioux line the brow of the hill, and pause there, a long wall of armed and mounted warriors come at last, feathered and bitter. They assemble at the top of the road's Z, that can be seen between the barn's corrugated roof and the manorhouse's thatch, the frame depending as ever on position and perspective, and so forth. The Oglala are in full regalia, for war, and have no business here. Slowly they advance down the hill, entering the yard in sulky silence, where they dismount. They stand about in groups, some sitting on the ground, some remaining on their horses, some leaning on the wooden fence. One of them knocks on the kitchen door and demands a hostage. They are sent to the barn to wait. In the kitchen we draw straws to decide who will be hostage. We play elaborate simulation games. We play for time. The Lakota, with good reason to trust no one, will not leave their horses outside, and take them into the barn, crowding in at the blacked out dark. When the barn is full of the Sioux with their horses, we sneak out and shut the door. They will not be able to open it from the inside, just as he could not, just as I could not, just as we could not, none of us in our turn to be locked in. Just to be sure, we nail the door up from the outside.

The barn, having stood some eight hundred years in the one spot, shudders, grunts, and slowly rears up, pulling its long taproots out of the ground. It shakes, as if waking from long barn sleep, hovers unsteadily awhile getting its legs, buried so long down under the farmyard. The barn's legs glisten, white, fluorescent, as the barn backs up into the yard, pausing only to clean itself with its long legs front and back as it arches over, and then slowly lumbers off up the road, up the hill to the summit, the Sioux weeping and hollering inside it.

Third frame:

Hollering: surely another Americanism? Three jets scream in low at thirty feet, scouring the brain. We're all dead again. We're all meaty burned lumps scattered over the landscape. We pick ourselves up, and fix our limbs back. What were we talking about?

On my sleeve the dragonfly, there one instant, gone the next, leaving no sign of his departure. Moved quicker than the eye can pick up, his going like the lines between the frames of the movie.

'There is an old proverb that says: *don't try to do two things at once.* This is the story of a boy who tried it. While employed as a moving picture operator in a small town theater he was also studying to be a detective.' This quotation comes to you from Keaton's *Sherlock Junior*, and is no doubt copyright, which is hereby acknowledged.

He would not see her, she would not see him. He would not write to her, she would not write to him. He would not telephone her, she would not telephone him. There would therefore be no ensuing narrative of love, betrayal, long misery and subsequent death. Nothing would happen. He would continue studying to be a detective, while earning his living as a projectionist.

This one stretched out, baking in the sun. These two making cherry tart and custard in the kitchen. That one asleep, apparently, and these others still suffering from target practice, and in the upstairs room Ms Buttercup pounding her typewriter into submission on the fifth draft. Some gone to the pub, and one of them visible walking up the concrete road, vanishing at the top. Another in the barn inventing new names for everyone else. And as the months passed the projector rolling, movie after movie.

111

Fourth frame:

He sits in the small office, looking through the lower right hand window pane in his line of vision from the desk. This is frame three: the spider laced glass beyond which is frame two aligned by barn wall right and house wall left, between which is frame one: the hill, the road snaking up.

Or down.

They took barn rubbings. They invented ancient and wise old sayings. They thought up original traditions and customs of the neighbourhood. They dug up their first living memories. They wrote blessings and curses. They designed strange new machines. They considered other evolutionary possibilities than the situations they found themselves in, and concluded God a dull inventor. They dreamed up fictional biographies for themselves. They invented dreams for each other. They coined old sayings for the forefathers of the hamlet.

At dinner everyone was to pretend to be someone else.

For myself I long for the simpler days, when you could get into the pictures with 2 jamjars and a halfpenny.

Well I don't care much to explain myself or things much he said, looking at everything through his glasses and his camera lens. He hadn't brought any film. I don't understand she said. Well, he began. With hindsight we'll see differently still. I don't know where we are. She was hot in reply: but you're supposed to know. In any case just tell me where I get my poems published. I don't know that either he told her. Another jet strafed them, there and then not there, like the dragonflies. They picked themselves up again, went into the kitchen. He took a small glass of cider, very dry, and sat at the table. Well? she demanded. He noted the tomatoes in the large can were a brand known as *Fantasia*. Tin, she said. Can's American. And laughed, surprised at her little joke, relaxing a little, her pencil poised for his list of publishers who would give their eyeteeth to publish her. An arm and a leg. Freshly baked scones from the oven, home made strawberry jam and thick Devon cream. He should be so lucky. And so should I.

Fifth frame:

He is not quite Buster Keaton, he is the protagonist, the projectionist, studying to be a detective. Very well then. From the projection box he crosses the auditorium between the halves of the watching audience. He climbs onto the piano, startling the pianist, faltering a moment, playing on. He climbs up into the cinema screen, a white sheet on a whitewashed wall. Bits of gilt and plaster flake off under his boots, but he's in there where everything is now fifty years ago where the farm was a farm in use with chickens and workmen, but he finds himself standing on a rock in the middle of a seamless ocean, and there's no farm hereabouts. He scratches his head in bafflement and turns to scan the horizon: he's standing on the one green tile in the dining room floor that first took his attention, he's standing on the great oak table but the table is hovering alone in empty space. He steps off holding his nose as if dropping into water, and is in another room, looks round bewildered and is standing on the log in the front garden, is standing on the chimney of the house, the crest of the hill where the road dips through, he is standing on a chair in a house in a distant city in another country where he finds himself looking over a screen into another room where a pretty young woman dressed in the style of the times is taking her clothes off, and has spotted him peeping, and is hurling a shoe at him. But before he can speak to say he knows nothing he's off again, he's in Africa, he's in Saudi Arabia, he's in Kentucky discussing Gurdjieff with the likes of you and you and you.

Keaton quotes:　　*I never thought you'd make it.*

*Father sent me to tell you
we've made a terrible mistake.*

*Be careful
or one of us will get hurt*

He stares back out of the frame of the screen. The audience are all out there, having paid their two jamjars and a halfpenny to come in. They're expecting a story. He scratches his head. From between his teeth he plucks dragonflies, arrows, old bones, a severed hand, marshmallows, Zulu warrior spears.

Sixth frame:

A story then: about Spain and the horses. About Punchinello. About the green tile in the dining room on which the murder weapon lay, centuries ago, the room and the oak table awash with blood and human meat. About a dream we had, about division. Or a story set in Trinidad, in which a soldier returns late to his barracks one night, very drunk. On the way he falls into a ditch, which being dry and he in drink, he decides to sleep in. Along the ditch comes an anaconda. As he sleeps it swallows his lower half, then it too goes to sleep. In the morning the soldier wakes, finding himself half digested in the anaconda. Now what happens? Get out of that.

You with the gumshoes. You with the old toffeepapers in your back pocket.

True or untrue, it's true enough. Things happen. Down the concrete roadway come the tanks, the hordes of refugees from the south, the deputation from the revolutionary committees, the spokesperson for the occupying forces, the liberators, the emissaries of King Cyrus, assorted bands of condottiere, sundry irregulars and counter revolutionary units disbanded but not disarmed, the camp followers and carpet baggers and the canteens and the film crews, a mob of characters not even fictional, and last the Sioux, not yet eliminated. The grass grows without explanation, and the birds fly without explanation. A wheel rolls down the hill, slowly following the curves of the road, without any sort of explanation whatsoever. And then a white Ford truck is about to arrive in the yard, bringing in the ambassador from reality, who must be fed and entertained.

We take the last frame out, there is no order and no magic, the events swallowed back into the world, the tile into the dining room floor, the one dragonfly now indistinguishable from the others on the river, Red Cloud and his people gone back into history bitter as ever, the film back into the can and the can lying now with others in the back of the white Ford truck.

114

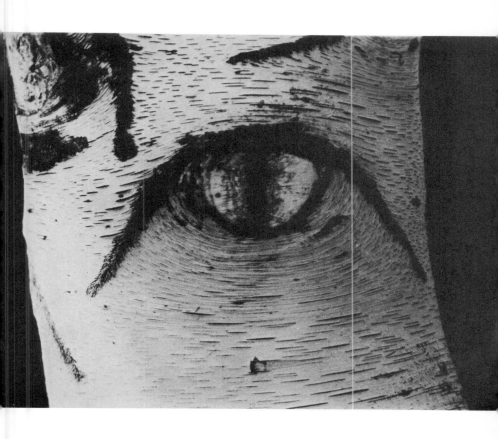

Ektachrome

Next door's yard full of bricks and bikes, neatly arranged: the blue drainpipe, the blanket over the kitchen end with the new door still waiting to be fixed. Above that, in the upstairs flat, a woman in a white brassière lifting breakfast plates, pausing at the vision of herself in what must be a mirror to her right above the sink, neither of which I can see from here.

To grow up as a child in that room where the taps project above the bottom of the window: in his first image of the world outside the room there they were, always in the foreground, prominently figured.

Above the houses the long body of the swan streaming back towards the river, gulls in the civic daylight, the ravens of the shopping precinct, sparrows, ducks, club footed proletarian pigeons, three crows, magpies whitening the early morning park: the birds of the river crossing.

Shaves, hunched into the mirror, glimpsing the yellow curtain, the shelf of bottles and jars, the dirty little cupboard behind the mirror where the shaving gear lives. Other places under the stairs that have not been looked into lately, dark corners where who knows what may be stored. Today I shall go out into the city, where I am a citizen, where I am known, where I have paid my rates after the usual warnings and the usual summons, and the television licence just before the ultimate visit of the inspector who confesses, when we discuss the matter, to a large collection of Buddy Holly 78s, as he crosses me off his hit list.

Half way through the film she turned to him and said in the dark 'you know you've only been sick once in all the time I've known you'. 'How extraordinary' he replied, and nothing further as they watched the rest in silence.

On the waste ground picks up an old halfpenny, green and pitted, surprised to recall how big they were. Aye, there was an empire, the legions from Dalmatia cursing their way across the river here, in the seaward wind. Nothing worth having: yellow plastic blowing through the immaculate caravans of the fairground people. Avoids the approaching meths man, and glowers at the hulk of St Thomas station, a Brunel back of envelope sketch, the stockholders pressing for a completion date. The trains pass for elsewhere.

Two years miserable Jack Gissing lived in the city, describing them amongst the worst, but recalling moments of rare content in his self absorption, walking the canal, passing the first pound locks in England.

The Portuguese, the Countess Isabella, long ago chained the river to force shipping to her own harbour downstream at Topsham, some time during the long generations her family schemed to control the city always slipping just beyond its grasp. The city's answer: the canal that Gissing walked, its curves glittering through the watermeads.

He will cross town he thinks beside the caravans of the fairground people. He will cross town he considers amongst the cinders and the broken bottles. He will cross town he decides amongst the closed amusement arcades, the tarpaulins and cables and generators and oily puddles, the line of open mouthed harlequins and the coconut shies, the image of the fat lady palm reader he's never visited. He will cross town.

Winos sleep along the river. Days here are necessarily slow. Not much is expected of anyone.

Nothing nothing nothing: the blackberries greasy from the railway, the apples and pears wormy, the lumpy detritus of abandoned vehicles. 'So what do you think of my sleeping with your wife?' Puffadder asks. *Not much. Are you asking me or telling me?* was all I said then, in my head honing the axe in my hand.

At the midpoint of the bridge I throw the halfpenny into the river for the passage. I take the river spirit seriously, and humour her. Turning right across the head of the bridge I tell imaginary tourists by the restored medieval causeway how the builder and his wife lie buried at their own request in one of the piers. A singular and secular engineer. For years a crazy woman lived on the causeway intimidating travellers and interfering with trade from the west. There was a problem with supplies into the city. They lived here, in tenements and hovels packed close together in the muddy river lees just below the town's western gate: dyers, tanners, thieves. Landed at Brixham, King Billy crossed it with his retinue and men-at-arms into the first city in England. So much for its *semper fidelis* motto. But a bride's city, I tell the tourists, imaginary as they are. The King's gift on marriage to his Queen, that surrendered neither her nor itself either to the Conqueror camped at the East Gate nor to the Parliamentarians camped later all around. Hoskins records how the citizens raspberried the Conqueror and gave him the bird sign and the thumb and fingers. For which he had the eyes of a hostage put out before the watching citizens. I leave the travellers with that information, and go up into the city, about my proper business.

Boats there'll be, son, and black swans along the estuary, and small wading birds. Later. I inspect the Roman footings of the Saxon wall the Danes broke when they wintered in the town and burned it. Beyond the townwall twenty centuries of rainy ploughland lie above the crossing, hills glimpsed by the townsmen, whatever they were doing with knives or money that made history.

Months later I return, and stand again by the sandstone hulk of the Brunel Atmospheric Railway pumping station, recognising it again. I turn the axe in my hand. I will go up town, amongst those who called themselves my friends, and put the axe in my enemy's skull.

It is a small hand axe, used for chopping kindling. The shaft is split, and bound with string along its length. Today I shall invest in a new shaft, and burn the old one in the stove. It will temper the blade, which I shall sharpen on the back door step.

Amongst old photographs of the former bridge one shows an overturned tramcar across the lines. The townspeople, gathered to see the accident's outcome, turn half towards the camera of the news photographer who may be presumed to be at that moment crouched under the black cloth of his apparatus. They have seen the nineteenth of these centuries here in the city change to the twentieth, the coming of electric light, bells ringing in celebration through the narrow streets. Another photograph shows the bridge before that bridge: the river flat and gray one louring afternoon that has faded further into the poor print of the postcard, sent by Miss White to her friend Mrs Sweetland. In another picture men lean outside the bar that stood at the far end of the bridge, where before that the church of St Thomas had been, from the tower of which after the Western Rebellion the parson was hung in all his vestments and popish ornament for siding with the rebels. As they besieged the western gate to which the causeway led the citizens opened the sewers downhill against them. So much for history, happening in the same place as these gulls. Crossing the bridge at speed I catch the moiré effect of the railings, and sight the town above the river.

Swans move, their white bulks flying low above the houses. In his yellow hat and the old jacket and jeans, with less than a pound in his pocket and a long way to go till Friday, he negotiates the traffic. It is a slow day for Lefty.

Crossing the river. Its name means water, fishing place. Back through Europe into Asia other rivers share its name, left by a people calling themselves *people of this land*, the Keltoi enduring at the fringes of the

119

Atlantic Water: *Isc.* In the new speech of the Latins was the same sound, meaning fish: *pisces.* Exe, Axe, Usk, Ox, Is, Ouse, Oise, Iscander: the river names proliferate, wherever the Celts had been. Uptown I shall use again their word for water, *uisque,* and sit to drink it in the Alpha Café, awaiting my moment.

'Since my wife isn't here' he said, 'would you happen to know where she put my sweater?' He boiled the water, prepared tea, made as if to go out into the yard but appeared to change his mind, and sat down facing me. 'You know the kind' he began, 'the sort of bloke that hangs out by the suspender belt counter in Marks & Spencers.' He stirred his tea. In my head I was thinking of other things. In my head I was flying from Bangkok to Delhi, one of the smoothest flights I'd ever had, but when I looked outside we were still on the ground and it was engine failure. He poured more tea. His house was a museum to things that never happened. In it his nights grew longer. 'If in doubt give it a good brushing down' he said. 'That's my motto. The swine. The pile of filth.' I wanted to tell him not to worry, but he forestalled me. 'I'm not worried about him' he concluded. 'He's nothing. I've seen better on a card of buttons.'

The audience grows impatient: on the screen nothing is happening, the film is blank, the narrative untold, the beam of yellow light enlarging dust specks, coat hair, lint, the soundtrack carrying no more than an occasional crackle of static. The shadow of a midge, if midge it be, skips across the lit space amongst the whorls of cigarette smoke, but it is not part of the movie and may be eliminated with a rolled up newspaper, or swept out of the door that opens from time to time to admit late comers. The audience grows restless.

Late at night in the Curry House I'm introduced to Jack. Jack is drinking, just like me, after hours. *Hello Jack* everyone says. Jack shakes hands all round, buys a bottle of Chianti, tells us all he'll go to jail rather than pay *her* his maintenance. Sure Jack. Sure you will. Jack talks of this and that, and comments on my cigarette, a Gauloise: 'is that the real thing?' *What real thing, Jack? Been on the force long have you, Jack?* Now there's a name to conjure with at midnight amongst the after hours taverns of the town. Jack. But don't take any notice of me Jack. I'm only drunk. I'm only working. I'm only here to shift the chandelier. Just like you Jack, I work everywhere. I'm always working, even now. Why when I'm asleep I feel the time is wasted unless I'm dreaming. It's in my nature. I'm an English Protestant. Jack.

Beneath the main street shards of Norman and Saxon. Beneath them stones laid by Vespasian's legionaries. Beneath that the ancient trackway following the ridges out of the hinterland to the river crossing.

The last of Leofric's Donation, 900 years later, frayed, thumbed, chopped, slashed, faded, burned, ringed by a wine glass, its speech foreign now, converted to some Christianity by a dull homilist, and the sight marks of the scribe picked out along the page's right hand edge much as a ploughman sights on the hawthorn, the book of the Wanderer in its fireproof metal trunk may be viewed between the hours of 2 and 5 on Mondays Wednesdays and Fridays in the library of the cathedral, in *Isca Caestra, Escanceaster, Exeter.*

Cuckoo's dirge drags out my heart.

Postcards of the old town, sent between Miss White and Mrs Sweetland. Other views from the Sweetland sons, from Cornwall where they went one summer on their bicycles, from Lambeth, and one from a honeymoon in Minehead, a window of a boarding house marked with a cross. And the last dated cards from France where they died, amongst the bloody butchery.

At noon in the bar the regular motley: bikers dressed as Storm Troopers, some disguised as sharpshooters, some as saints, some as army veterans ashamed of their wars, one as Jesus of Nazareth with his girlfriend Moll Flanders. Money, jukebox, gambling machine. It is the typical interior of a bar in the later twentieth century of this part of the globe, it is dinnertime in this bit of the galaxy. I order whisky. A young man comes in, dressed as the Mad Hatter, blue tails and tie and top hat, his girl as Lauren Bacall. *You know how to whistle Steve?* she says. *Just put your lips together and blow.* Everything she says is scripted. Everyone is dressed as someone else, derived from other images or other times and other places via the movies and the newsreels and the pages of books, but amongst the potential violence certain conventions apply. Otherwise for more than an hour there's all this entertainment, for a few English pound notes. I consider it a bargain.

Later it would be a drowned city, meaning not a city underwater where the drifting bells of the citizens float upward at midnight and on certain days the clocks of the churches can be heard booming in the dark water, but a metaphor: a town lost to a particular man, the history being of myself. Though he may return here he will find it not particular: just another town, another destination, another departure. If he recognises

121

a face it is older and stares through his, and knowing the time it would take to introduce himself anew to one who was once a brother, he doesn't bother. Some stones, some corners, certain cafés, the clay tile pigeons and the painted bishops on the crests of buildings, catch his eye again where his life ran sometimes sweet in the burgh, where all are drowned now. Besides, he has an errand. He has an axe. He has a train to catch later, and will be sure not to miss it.

And if it's not departure it's arrival. If it isn't liquid it must be solid. If it isn't fiction it's fact. If it isn't the metropolis with squats and bedsits and the impending divorce of some lady I live with who won't let me play her record player because all her records remind her of her late lover departed for Valparaiso and never said why and in any case died trying, then it's the sullen suburban life of the provinces, of my imaginary brother in Birmingham with his wife and kids and his job down at Failure & Co., and his spare room he grudgingly lets me use from time to time. And either turns out to be fiction. Reality out here in the universe turns out more desperate, where only I know what it feels like to me here beneath my waistcoat and watch chain.

I consider my errand: the planting of the axe along the parting of my enemy's hair. Here on this planet, in this sector of the great universal nowhere I find myself towards the end of the eighth decade of the century, shy of violence, avoiding faction, wary of causes, awkward amongst contention, arriving on a day return to the city I lived in some years, on this particular errand: to kill a particular man. I want to kill him, with my little axe for cutting firewood, and piss on his grave. And he knows it.

Therefore I need do nothing further.

In the town of the wanderer, beside the river and the western gate, where I might have lived, grown old and died. Or in some other place.

This morning when the wind chopped the surface of the river into small slapping waves repeating the river's sound in the mnemonic of its name: *isc isc isc*, I considered my obsession with the crossing place, with other tongues that crossed here: dog Latin, Dalmatian, Gaulish, Celtic, miscellaneous Gothic and Germanic gutturals, monosyllabic Saxon, brief clatter of Danish, Norman, Church Latin, King Billy's Dutch, and the various English of this my consideration of the crossing telescoped from the creole of those times into these transactions at the river.

In the cathedral I visit Isabella and her Lord, laid in sweet effigy together, sundry bishops, Sir John Speke. The space maintains itself through the centuries, a great stone worn by the backsides of the former citizenry, some of whom have left their initials. Outside the sunlight smacks the towers, and Hooker's statue sits open-booked, a pigeon on his cap, as usual. An event, or its portrait, summer, early afternoon, northern hemisphere.

Tourists snap their cameras: where a dean was knifed, where a mayor hanged for it, where Drake the pirate boasted his mouth, where a woman burned for refusing the vernacular prayer book, to each their moments. The ground conceals shopkeeper hoards of outdated currency, the hooped rib bones of soldiers and monks unflowering beneath the archaeologists' trowels and brushes. In 1918 at the Armistice the cathedral overflowed to fill the space around itself with townsfolk singing *Rock of Ages*, a moment certain as any other, as certain as the rebel peasants standing centuries before in the same space with halters round their necks expecting death, as certain as this moment.

Not everything surely she said, halfway through the movie. What's that you say? He was in the dark, concentrating. Not everything is significant, soaked in meaning, chafing to be understood. *Quite so* he agreed. They were shushed silent. In the film the belts and pulleys and drive shafts and gears of some vast unexplained machinery clanked in the rain beside the road beside a white building beside a tree beside a woman feeding white chickens from her apron beside a red wheelbarrow beside a white bearded man beside a pitchfork.

Picture of Joe who asked me to make him one. Joe, who is dead now. Joe who was billed as a boxer for his slanted eyes and ochre skin fresh off the boat from Siam, the young bantam cock. But Joe's accent and birthplace was Plymouth. He was amateur champion, but for fighting in the boxing booths for money he was banned for life. Joe in the ditch in his good shoes and snappy suit in the muck showing some chippy how to weld pipe, kids to feed, wife gone long ago and killed in a car with another man, and later another woman he courted for years who never arrived at the registry office but married another man elsewhere on the same day, same hour. And Joe with three trolleys of Christmas groceries walking past the checkout at Tesco, no one saying a dicky. They told him at the hospital the pain he complained of was an ulcer. But it was cancer of the liver. He died. I didn't visit. This is instead of. I think he turned his face to the wall and groaned and declared he'd had enough of everything, and died.

The bus crosses the river, where the sky opens and the long cloud beyond the stand of poplars is the smoke of a giant train, and the river curves seaward out of the north. In the town the landscape glimpsed down streets becomes abstractions again: maps, mileage charts, tourist information, county histories, camera settings, destinations announced at stations, signposts, motorway exits, etymologies of place names, geographies, items on the agendas of busy local government officials, the contents of these files.

The feet of the effigy of Countess Isabella, she that chained the river and the river's trade. Her feet rest on two stone swans whose crossed necks are chained to their haunches that they might never fly. Their intertwined necks represent a description of sorrow. But not, I think, for her.

Where I might be, collecting my apocrypha, remarks overheard and scribbled on bits of paper stuffed into my back pocket, lost most of them though some surface in the lamp's glare into ehrhardt italic; it is a small justification for the privilege of existing at all on the earth, visiting the marriage museum, consorting with the little sisters, bobbing up and down upon the reefs of mundane disasters to tell a joke, refuse advice, ignore a jib, report a scandal, overhear from the next bench the occasional obscene confession, organise my strategy for surviving the collapse of domesticity by hanging on to my raft of an Adler typewriter, tapping out this long long sentence cheating all the way, resorting to the common comma as the line stretches out towards the horizon.

I live in language as in water, swimming for my life.

I visit the wife, the ex-wife. And will she make a carrot cake, and three-cornered egg and watercress sandwiches, tempting me with talk of chicken vol-au-vent and scrubbed children and newly baked bread? Or will she witter about her lover, ex-lover, the aforementioned Puff-adder, the subject of the sharp little axe I carry in my business man's briefcase? Perhaps she can be got to plant it in his skull, on her behalf, and mine.

Insufficient information available. Reprogram. Check. Check entry data. Re-enter. Offer me a cup of tea, woman, and what little news that comes from her enchanted realm. I'm only visiting. She moves objects around in what is now her kitchen, opens and closes the door of *her*

124

fridge, attacks the crockery in *her* sink unit, makes the usual domestic noises, performs her territorial dance, the eternal wifely dust raising ceremonies, and makes a pot of lapsang souchong. Little news from the event horizon. A failed negative experience, our marriage, as they call it out on Long Island. *So how are you?* she enquires, and I look behind me to see who she's talking to. I sit facing the open doorway to the hall, mistaking the door frame for a mirror in which I find myself unreflected.

I'm from the invisible planet. I'm from the nether world where most of us just fail to be, living out our lives in fractions, our fingers slithering away from each other. Behind me the unconscious yawns away into eternity.

Goodbye.

Goodbye city.

No good at anything I overhear, and look down at my shoes, two in number, one for each foot striding one before the other as I cross the bridge for the last time. At midpoint I look round to be sure no one sees me, and drop the axe in the river, the axe in the Exe. I should have stayed where it was safe in the Land of Pink. I should have gone to Birmingham. I should have been a Trappist. I should have gone to London, 20 years ago. I should have joined the navy for life and come out about now to a gratuity and a workable trade, barring accidents. And Exocets. I should have become a programmer and paid my dues and joined the interesting people who do exciting twentieth century things.

Otherwise the gull's lift, river's turn, wind's work on stone, frost's message: *I have news for you: deep red the bracken.* Otherwise mine is a feeling of being always on the wrong side of the river, arriving on the wrong day in the wrong suit of clothes carrying the wrong currency and can't find my passport and all the banks closed, a national holiday of indeterminate length in some ancient southern town, the sunlight dusty on the boulevards. And then the flags begin crumbling in the churches, then the grass on the hills around the town turning yellow. Then the signs all in another language directing the tanks and the infantry, singing a jolly marching song and not (thank you very much Raworth, thank you very much Bogart) not thinking very much of anything but wondering about supper and who they will shoot tomorrow.

Chickenshit I overhear, at last on the bridge's other side. *It don't make chicken salad.*

Stolen: everything. Everything borrowed, everything blue, one magpie for sorrow: these words, gut sounds, ur exclamations, belly moans, Chainstoke's breathing, birth pangs, primal howls, snarls of rage, whines of complaint, long nursed mutterings, whimpers, bronchial whispers, arthritic groans, yells of frustration, remarks off or in passing, orgasmic gatherings of sound from far back in the fourteenth century of the throat, the dark ages of the chest, the tenth century of the thrusting backbone, the iron age and stone age and misty cave grunts rising from the belly's pit as she comes at last, the last whimper the last survivor of the ark on Ararat and the last ebbing of the flood. All stolen. And she sleeps, I sleep, we sleep, the world sleeps, the entire creation may cool off for a while for all we care. It's over, or didn't happen, or was merely a passing notion in the back brain of the supposed creator of it all, who seems not to be about at the moment, and hasn't left a note saying *Gone to lunch.*

The bus climbs the hill. The sunlight begins to fail, blazing out at the moment of decline, striking down the river valley, gold again among the rooftops. I have a train to catch, and these distractions must be let go. On the upper deck of the bus I pay my fare and think about the splash of the axe striking the dull water of the river.

Invisible thread

The blinding

He has returned from the country of defeat, carrying a fish spear and a bone axe, an antler, a white stone with a hole through it: his trophies.

The grave-goods lie on the ground before him. One by one he touches them with a finger, speaking for each the names they are known by, the names of the people who shaped them from stone and stone-melt, who were at the last buried with their tools and ornaments. The wind carries off the names, folding them all into itself.

The dead are here he says, in the old tongue. With his hands he describes the coming of light to the plains, the first trees of birch and arctic willow springing between the fingers of retreating glaciers. He speaks of the first deer caught by the hunters, weighted with stones and thrown into the river. Here, on the ridge of brown shale, the migrants stood, the man with his chisels, the woman with the firebox pressed to her breasts.

He knows the month the first creatures noticed the stars and began to count and name them, shaping them in groups to make the animals of their stories painted in the deep caves of the ancestors. Long after, he says, men built towers by piling stones to get closer to the sky of stars. His feet leave prints in the mud. Later, coming back, he is surprised, discovering his footsteps again, printed in the stone.

I am Jacob

Each moment, just as it is, and already we're in trouble. I am Jacob, trapped in the hologram of myself. There are no names for anything or anyone. There are only so many nights at the Mirabelle, so many songs, so much wine, so many dances, so many loves. *Unbounded possibilities are not given to man. If they were his life would dissolve in the boundless.*

*

I am Jacob, arguing with stones, setting out memorials and covenants, deceiving with the skins of kids and in my turn deceived, taking a stone for a pillow and dreaming of a ladder from heaven. I labour seven years for him who deceives me, then seven more and seven more and still he deceives me, my master. I am the fool. I stole my father's blessing from my brother. I am in flight, as ever.

*

The band plays. It makes unbelievable music that renders everyone in the room unconscious so that in sleep I sleep more deeply, in dreaming I fall into a further dream, where I am making love with my woman. Another woman comes in, and stops the music. It is too sweet, too wonderful, she says. It is too much for us. The band plays again, but with caution. Now they are self-conscious, uninspired. We are waiting for the great music to come back, but it doesn't. It seems unlikely now that these indifferent musicians might ever have made such music. I begin sketching the woman, she who stopped the music. She is in a drawing that already exists, somewhere, her legs and feet merge there with a stream. I am only vaguely copying what already exists. She is the blank spaces in the drawing. She is the white paper. A man comes in. He is her husband, suspicious of her being there, angry that she has sent the youngest of her children away. I hide the drawing that will not be finished now. They are quarrelling. The band plays on.

*

And in the city the massed police sirens play the national anthem, the flowers in the windowboxes rustle like money, the office blocks purr and hum, and the ministers promise to tell no more lies. On the TV in the background the President is limbering up to show all the world and everyone in it he's good for another term. For an old man, he's made up to look young, when what we might be hoping for in one so old is wisdom. For so much power, he's not very bright. It seems that those who hold power are thereby unfit to use it, and whoever appears on TV must pretend to be somebody else, and speak only as an imaginary character, a projection. The President has a hint of cowboy about him, and the look of business. He is an old ham actor, mouthing lines he doesn't understand written by several hands, as they come up on the prompter, and we are all his toys. Everyone in the world is his enemy, divided between the hostile powers each armed sufficient to obliterate everything living. Mere minutes lie between this man's command and oblivion, between the missiles in their silos and their targets in these downtown streets of Kiev, Detroit, Utrecht, Surbiton. The President is lifting weights, flexing his muscles and his smile. The President is shaking hands with everyone in snowy Cedar Rapids, and promising he'll deal with the other side. But neither side will talk to the other. They're like two boys sticking their tongues out saying *he started it*. Now

129

they won't even play marbles together, or water polo, or run in the three-legged race. Or am I dreaming again?

*

I am Jacob. I hate my brother. He is gross, vulgar, crass, thick, selfish, hairy, foul-mouthed, ignorant. I am ashamed of him. In my dream I kill him. I hit him over the head with a brick or a bottle, there's so much blood I can't tell, and push his battered body out of the window. In the kitchen there's blood everywhere. I begin cleaning it up, planning out my story: *it was an accident. My brother fell out of the window onto his head, I bear his memory along with me in grief, forever.* But he staggers back into the room, not dead. He's groggy, bloody, not yet aware I hit him and pushed him out. Perhaps he's brain damaged and dependent on me now for the rest of our days, worse than before. I have put myself in his power.

*

All night I wrestled with the angel, who did not prevail against me, till at first light I would not let him go until he blessed me. He gave me a new name and a new secret. But I was hit in the hollow of my thigh, and my thigh out of joint. I am Jacob, who stole one blessing and fought for another, but I am always one leg out of kilter.

*

Poor Jacob. There are only so many nights, the lights glittering in the desert, the wells blocked by stones, the mirages travelling the landscape, and nowhere to escape the surveillance of the high reconnaissance and the random targetting of the computers. I am pinned in a glass case, an example. There are only so many rungs on the ladder, so many stones, so many blessings, and only one encounter with the angel. For each moment a stone raised, a heap of boulders for the final standoff with Laban. And for the wound in the hollow of the thigh the orthodox in memory do not eat *that meat of the sinew that shrank.* Centuries pass. Jacob and all his sons and daughters are mixed in with the weather.

*

In China, in Shanghai, in the tenth century of the Christian reckoning, a group of Jacob's descendants settled. Another thousand years passed. Today there are few of them, the community dwindling, yet their name in Chinese still means *those who do not eat the leg.*

See: I am Jacob.

*

130

Dreaming of horses

As usual: silence, deeper than the steep and stoney road down into the valley. Always the same sort of place, a valley bottom overgrown with trees and weeds the sunshine fades in: a shaft of gold lancing the fern in the clearing, beyond that wilder country. This is where I am, usually, in the same dream that comes back again. There is water, a stream's makings among loose rocks and glacier scourings, moving through the valley's upturned apex where the steep sides meet, and I and the water meander. And off the road, by the stone bridge where the track turns sharp to take the uprise, the abandoned buildings. They are dangerous, of course, crumbling walls and collapsing stairways, loose floors, flaking plaster, great funnels of spiderweb. And there I look for things, souvenirs, objects I might have lost, or someone hidden. Or I hide things. Or I find them again. I make secrets in these falling rooms. Long ago, in some time I can't remember, I might have lived here.

I dream of the wild huntsman. With a companion I have encountered one of his pack of brown beagles, and my friend shot at the dog to drive it off. I took the gun from him, firing its bullets into the ground, but the huntsman, angry, returns with his pack and now we are hunted and have no weapon, hiding in these old buildings, blocking flimsy doors with wormeaten furniture. My companion, my friend no more, runs off. I'm calling *not me not me he did it* when the huntsman in his red coat astride the great shining horse with all his hunting dogs bursts through the doors, and last I hear him muttering through gritted teeth: *Not him. We've come for you.*

The moments come back, in their ferocity. I am seven, at Grisethwaite on the Thirsk road. Hills to the southeast age into blue, and on them is the white horse cut into the hillside. It is always there on our skyline, like a medal, shining through the broad lands of the northmen. One day on a holiday we set out on bicycles to reach it, but never got there. A girl fell down a hill and sat bleeding from the head on an ant nest, and we turned back. The moments return, my life a vague construction of them, made of points towards which everything tends and beyond which everything is altered.

Kairos.

The great plough horse is on his back, his four legs kicking, screaming in panic. He can't rise again, and is afraid. Tilly, the landgirl, stronger

131

than any man dithering around the perimeter of flailing limbs, moves in ahead of them. The horse is rolling from side to side, screaming. She calls to him. She dives, she croons to him, she wrestles with the horse to turn him, hugs him, holds him, rocks him and rolls him on to his side and he rises at last and stands, shivering, lathered, hard breathing, feral. In his great flaring teeth he is clutching a long brown hank of hair, bloody at the end that is a patch of Tilly's scalp yanked out. She is bleeding. The men are ashamed.

I know this road. Soon there will be the descent into whimsy, the pretty village, the place I repeat myself again and again and stand around with a glass of punch, trying to imagine conversation. What do people talk about? Up there no doubt there will be a tavern with lights and music and some cheer, called say *The New Delight, The Hope Revived, The Prospect*, selling good ale and pasties and thick doorstep sandwiches, the landlord and the missus cheerful even when they fight, telling long stories late into the night, long after closing time. But I will never reach it, though soon enough there will be the usual demands for narrative and common sense, and rather than frame my damp squib of a tale I'll turn back. Soon enough.

Everyone with a story he and she is telling him and herself every waking moment and then some in dreaming. The tale is long and rambling, full of detours and further explanations and boiling down in the end to nothing much but the want to talk and fill the air with voices. It begins at about age 5 and 7, when we have language to tell it to all who will listen even a moment in passing, and it goes on till death and the hardest of all is to stop telling it. Those who are worst off are those who have no story. Everyone's story is fascinating, even so, and often ravelled up like string, and we are each driven to tell it one way or another. Therefore we are devious in our ways of getting into the conversation, an ear and an audience and we're off. Given half a chance we are telling our tales, but mostly in silence, to ourselves. Imagine all of it aloud, the endless babble in our skulls with all our dialects and all we mean by words such as *love* for instance, *lonely, to grieve for*, and all we regret as we age and the tale tells out. Most of us, thank God, keep it to ourselves, the endless Who-I-am and What-to-say-of-it, the how and the why of Where-am-I-going and What-I-should-have-said, and so forth, with elaborations, footnotes, recapitulations, sub-texts, appended notes, exaggerations, lies. Mostly, thank all the gods, we're content to spell out our stories with the tips of our tongues on the roofs of our mouths, where no one

132

ever contradicts.

Or is there, somewhere in the universe, a place where all the unfinished sums turn up, and all the wrong calculations, and all the love affairs that never happened, never got started, or never worked out?

The buildings are as ever, deserted, dangerous. They are said to be haunted, out here in the woods, the hiding places of suicides and desperate lovers, forbidden by all the stern fathers of the district, sometimes a hangout for brave adolescents who have long ago broken all the windows. I am there with other men, working. Our work is furtive and efficient. We labour in and out the farm buildings, breaking into the basements, where for some reason a great quantity of coal has been stored. We don't know how much, there are other outbuildings further in the trees, among the whirls of briar and tangled chicken wire, and underneath them more cellars of black dusty coal, long mined and stored here, we don't know why. We don't know whether the coal belongs to anyone. We are perhaps stealing it to sell, or moonlighting on the dole, and it is for these reasons we are furtive, and not our fears of the buildings themselves. We have a cart, and today it seems I'm the carter, coaxing each cartload of coal up the steep road through the valley, and I am in charge, today, of the two horses, one black, one white, that do the work. Though I would rather be investigating the buildings, and would rather not be carting coal, I have an easy enough time of it, and I'm close with the horses, their sweat and their great breathing.

But the truth is, I am afraid. I am fascinated by the buildings, deserted long ago by their people, leaving all their furniture and implements, shirts in the drawers, salt in the cupboards, letters and demand notes in the desk, the last dated November 1934. I'm curious who lived there, for how many generations, who were they when they abandoned them. I want to get in and investigate, when the coal's out. I am afraid not of what I may find there, but of what it might tell me.

And then, suddenly and abruptly and without an explanation I walk off the job. Perhaps I'm going for a drink, or a walk in the woods, perhaps I'm weary of always doing one thing and wanting to do another. I leave the horses in their cart at the bottom of the hill, and my workmates heaving the coal out, and walk off. In a little while, ten minutes or so, I look back down the road, and of course it's my fault: the other men have walked off too, and are coming with me, and the two horses are suddenly in panic, tangled in the shafts of the cart, leaping against each other. I go back. I can't free them. I can't get close enough. It's too late. They are screaming, and the terrified kicking of their limbs drives me back, knowing they will injure themselves terribly, and will be killed, beautiful as they are. Never mind it is all my fault, now it is I who must kill them. I have a baseball bat in my hands, standing on a wall above the two plunging horses, and I am hitting the black horse and the white horse in turn over their frantic heads. I hit them again and again, as hard as I can, but something in me holds back the blow. However many times I hit them, I can't kill the horses.

Ripon revisited

So much for thirty years wandering. I'm back where I was at at nine and clumsy among buckets on the cobbled market, some Saturday noon. So much for all the years between. So much for my book of absences to be called variously *Young Wives Praying*, if not *No Hump Shunt* or is it *Razors supplied on request?* I'll never begin it, now. Small and awkward, I press my nose to the rainy picture house glass and read off the names of old movies, and the words painted on the town hall: *Except the Lord keep the citie, the watchman waketh in vain*. Not much changed: the stacked vegetables, the wooden taxi office like a Tyrolean chalet on iron wheels, the ironmonger's shovel sign, his window crammed with seeds and spades and white pot eggs and storm lamps. In the Double Luck Chinese Restaurant the menu announces to all that after ten on Fridays and Saturdays *no soups starters or sweets* will be served beyond the 31st March. This time around, the woman in blue says nothing. Evening plunges down on the town, in the bus station there's a soldier in battledress waiting for a bus, and a couple of kids with a transistor, and in the bar of the Unicorn a dark silent man wearing a silver razorblade at his throat, drinking to cool his anger. At nine the watchman blows the long horn at the square's four corners, and the young farmers are driving into town with their skinny young wives. They stand at the bar, the men talking to each other, and all the women go to the ladies together wearing their long green dresses and smiling, just as long ago in the movies.

134

Problems of a northern boyhood

Three men mow a meadow at time and a half for four hours of a September Sunday. One of them, the foreman, earns one tenth more than the other man, his brother, but the third man – but a boy out of school – earns one third less than the foreman, who is his uncle on his mother's side, but no matter. Between them they earn, cash in hand, £46.86, with which they will supplement their labourer's wages, with never a nod to the taxman. What is each man's hourly rate?

If the foreman invested his afternoon earnings in national savings bonds at 15% compound interest, how much would he be worth at the end of five years, and would he be worth mugging? If the youth gave most of his money to his mother for lodging and she bought bread, butter, jam, ham, spam, lamb and a wee dram would she see any change from a five pound note? And if the other man put his money on a horse running 17-1 in a race the next morning how much would he have won if he'd won, if the horse hadn't stumbled, the weather had held, the barley grown ripe and the farmer paid up, and what will he say to his wife?

Misericorde

North, we inspect the misericordes beneath the choir seats. They are fifteenth century carved bosses, most of biblical scenes, smoothed by the leaning backsides of generations of prelates, who but for these carvings stood chanting to their saviour. Eve is tempted by the serpent. The Israelites cross the Red Sea. One we cannot understand: seen from above one figure pushes another in a cart. It is the distant legend of a Saxon saint. In the eighth century this man lived in the far west on the edge of Dartmoor, where he was a shepherd. His father died, his mother sickened, he couldn't tend both her at home and his sheep in the field in a country of wild beasts. He put his mother in a wheelbarrow, supporting her with a strap about both their backs, she facing him, and wheeled her across southern England, as the carving records. At Steyning where the barrow fell to bits in Sussex, he built a chapel, and there the only church in his name still stands. For this he was made a saint. His miracles were mundane and capricious: walking by corn at harvest the serfs laughed at him with his barrow. He cursed them and brought down a great storm, ruining their crop. Presumably he and his mother were soaked, and how well she survived the downpour and the rough ride we're not told. There seems little logic to any of it. But consider these distances: a long journey from Devon to Sussex still currency as a tale to be carved in wood in North Yorkshire seven centuries later. Such a distance was Homer's from Troy. *Misericorde*: to have pity on the heart.

At the university

To hell with Ultramondanes, says the faculty banner. The students work in the singing buildings, studying strike ratio and zero option, still struggling for a unified field theory. On Level Six cures are being developed for new diseases being incubated on Level Seven. One department works to counteract the work of another. The computers posit languages of the future, which other computers decode. In the new wing professors are being plugged into the main services, and begin immediately holding seminars in Etruscan, Advanced Light Theory, and the work of minor Elizabethan sonneteers. The students are brushed down daily and topped out annually with diplomas. In revenge, one of them has sprayed the side of the buildings *concrete brain factory*. They have cracked the problems of the non recurring decimal, but because of the betrayal of the prime numbers all the codes are becoming useless, and they fear the loss of their secrets. Slight variables have been introduced into the value of pi. It is a dead end. Empires are being made out of stolen bathplugs. We are all disappointments to our parents. We have all let down our loves, denied brothers, sold our sisters on the market, betrayed friendship, been bought cheap. Here is the square in which the riots will take place, and here the offices where history is rewritten to exclude them, and here the broad steps on which the revolution will fail even to be recorded, its victims dumped in unmarked graves, its graffiti meticulously scrubbed out, a shopping complex built across the place of martyrdom. In the long soap operas of the future these events will never figure.

The poetry reading

The poet arrives to read his works, surprised to find the reading taking place in a busy department store, in a section set apart by screens on two sides about chairs and a podium, a glass of water, and the organiser who seems to be the sales manager for this floor. The poet is confused, and opens his briefcase to check his invitation. It seems there's a promotion under way, with huge discounts on household goods, they're in the haberdashery and there's a big offer on kitchen knives. Customers rush about with bargains in bedding and Crown Derby, it's like a tupperware party away from home. The loudspeakers play *Call me irresponsible* between announcements for spot bargains in other parts of the store, all in a fever of ringing tills. Somehow the poetry reading is part of the promotion, the sales manager murmurs, and adds it was his idea in the first place. He has always taken an interest in poetry, he says, as his hobby, and confides to the poet he has made a few honest efforts of his own. But perhaps they should go in now, he suggests. The reading is about to begin. The poet nods, looking at his contract, wondering if he's arrived on the right day, whether he's applied for a job here, whether this isn't really an interview. The salesman begins showing him the knives, of which they have a large selection. The poet grows more and more confused. *I didn't come here to sell knives* he says. The salesman shepherds him along the racks of knives, extending now along the insides of the screens where the reading is to be. *That's all right* the salesman says. *We're just about to start.* Sitting in the audience the poet sees almost everyone he ever knew or loved or fought at one time or another in different districts of his life. Most of them, he's pleased to note, don't know or recognise each other, though some know of each other through him. They are delegates from other times and places, but seeing them all at once he can't work out who anyone is. He can't match names to faces or faces to contexts, and now he must face them all. The salesman nudges his arm, glancing at his watch. *Shall we go in?* he says. *Or would you like to see some more knives?*

Magic liquid

More years pass, with indecent haste. Suddenly my children are grown in their own lives, seeing as they see, and I must be to them that man

137

who was to me *my father*: remote, mysterious, capable of grieving in the open. 'One day you'll wake up' he said. 'And you won't know what hit you.' He was right. One day I woke. Everything hit me at once. By then he was long dead, in no position to be told how right he'd been.

On the beach I imagine I will find everything I ever lost washed ashore. Eventually I will be knee deep in sixpences, marbles, hats, tin soldiers, books, biros, penknives, friends, tickets, lovers, my odes for Larry the Longlost, my notes from *Sexual behaviour under nuclear threat* by J.P. Benson. I ceased to love one wife, and as slowly began to love another. Every lie I'd ever told came home to accuse me, drunk, braying like donkeys. Years of silence were punctuated by punchups. I did a runner, became homeless, invented false names for myself, and more comfortable biographies. Nothing was saved from the wreck but my skin and what I could carry in two hands and my wandering skull: the tools of my trade, a pocketful of pencil stubs and scribbled backs of envelopes, paper bags, cheque stubs, enquiries from the taxman, and other communications from the gods.

Just words, notes out of context, quotations attributed to improper sources. I know for instance it was Spencer Tracy who said of some character *She wouldn't know beans with the bags untied.* But of whom, and in which movie? Who said *Don't ever act in a place they sell hard liquor?* And who said if anyone said *Don't make the port of Halifax in the winter time if you can make other arrangements, Captain?* Who?

The world is a four letter word. Tell God not to make any new sorts of animals. We'd only exterminate them. Some things you just know: that a spider in the bath means it's autumn.

And you, gentle reader, quite properly demand narrative, and ere long shall have one. Some way these words will muster into a tale, and here we have already a ship, a shipwreck, and a shore on which debris is looked for. It arrives in its own time and in no special order. When the wind drops there are loose phrases everywhere, chewed on the rocks, spiked on old boards, tangled with netting and snapped ropes, ripped open.

138

And other tales

All over England, jumping on and off trains, he sees her vanish round corners, it is never her in any case, it is someone he has invented, a woman's shape to fit his shape, travelling the same wavelength. He is selfish and at first his only ticket is his ego. Men begin in this way, as do women, some remain so till they die. It is not, he will slowly come to realise, a cosmic welfare state, but a very difficult place wherein the norm is danger, decay, defeat, destruction, death, and anything else beginning with D. As he travels he reads, occasionally glancing at the details of the landscape through the train window, and grapples with inertia, gravity, probability, ignorance, subjectivism, coincidence. It is enough, some days, just to remember who he is, his name and date of birth and other details, and his many destinations.

In any plot always leave one of the characters out. Especially the one who says *I told you so.*

And where is she, who will be his love, and the light to his dark shadow, flesh to his flesh, fire to his skin, and leave her brown odour on him ever after? We shall call her Marjorie. But she won't be anyway he expects. His act of imagining her defeats itself. She will occupy her own space, and won't wear shades to impress him or anyone.

On the train north he is reading a book and trying to understand the theory of relativity. The example given is of a man (such as himself) on a moving train whose own walking speed is derisory to the speed he and the train together are travelling, without notice. There is, he realises, thinking he glimpses someone who might be her standing with a bicycle at a road barrier, his walking speed as he goes to the buffet car. She was wearing a blue headscarf, a cotton dress, and was instantly gone forever. And there's the train's speed, and its relation with his own. Since the buffet car is forward and he is walking in the same direction as the train, is he in fact travelling faster than the train? And when he comes back to his seat with his coffee he believes he needs to counter his bafflement, will he be travelling more slowly? Several young women in the buffet are not her, nothing like her. And then he thinks about the Earth's rotational speed, its swing around its star, the star's speed around the axis of the galaxy and away from every other star, and then the galactic speed. All of this so far as he can figure becomes spiral motion. He finds this comforting. He finds the coffee comforting. He returns to his seat, opens up his book and reads *we know now that all matter is composed of waves of probability*, and tries to imagine that, and falls asleep, and dreams of her again. His non explicit lower body approaches her non explicit lower body. They are fucking at the speed of light, the molecular chains between them breaking and reforming, her face and all the stars a blur, as ever.

In his dream his cry is a cry falling head over heels through the universe, forever and forever. So far, that is, as he can be said to be falling, so far as anything can fall forever. All the same he is falling, flailing, desperate, no air to carry his cry, no last words from a choking man.

And in any case how long is forever, brothers and sisters? Not long in this case. Forever with us lasts only till Thursday week, when there will be a complete new dispensation, and with one mighty bound our protagonist will be free. And then it's Thursday afternoon. He stops falling through the cosmos, and wakes on a hazy Friday noon in summer. He's sprawled in a deckchair, and has been sleeping in the sun too long, and a thrush is puncturing what would otherwise be urban groan. His sweet peas are in flower. Bees are droning in and out of flowers. The song-thrush pleases him. He should be weeding, now he has so much time on his hands. He has been dreaming, and shakes his head to rid it of the dream of an unknown man on a train drinking coffee and then abruptly falling headlong through nothing. He yawns. He gets up from the deckchair. He never drinks coffee.

He crushes the greenfly on the sweet peas, resolving to squirt them with soapy water. He considers his life. He is an ageing and grumpy man, a widower, a senior ticket clerk in the railway booking office, he smokes rollup tobacco, he enjoys a glass of lager and the occasional cigar, he reads science fiction, enjoys watching cricket, takes a bath once a week, once a year goes to his sister's in Bognor Regis, eats fish on Fridays even though he's not a Catholic. He is a man of deeply established habits. He is pleased that his life is in order, and that he's not falling through the universe in that tedious fashion without any possibility of narrative action or dialogue and nothing to discover there, and he thanks God even the sweet peas and the greenfly have good reasons for being where they are.

He has no name.

He sits down to think about this in the deckchair. He thinks about his supper, cod or plaice. He thinks about his approaching retirement. He thinks about his dog, Manilla, asleep in the shadow of the deckchair.

He thinks about his dead wife, Marjorie, and his son Peter who never visits. The thrush departs. A cloud briefly crosses the sun. He falls asleep.

They meet and fall in love, they marry, they have children, they grow old, their children have children, they die. They meet, they fall in love, they don't marry, don't have children, or they do. They meet, they are already married, or one of them is, they part. They meet, they are already married, they leave their existing partners, there is grief, guilt, confusion, they marry each other. Or not. Or they lose each other, nonetheless. They meet someone else. They resolve to live alone. They die alone. They die in any case, abruptly, all on the same day, all over the world, huddled like the dead in the boat houses at Herculaneum.

Too bad.

He dreams he's invisible, a common enough dream. He can't see himself at all, and mistakes doorways for mirrors and wonders why he's missing. Apparently no one can see him either, except when he's reflected. Therefore he's obliged to carry a full length dressmaker's mirror around with himself. It's heavy and awkward, and the wheels are stiff, he can't take it on buses without an argument, and there are respectable hotels that won't admit him. He worries that if the wind catches his mirror it may break, it might even take someone's head off. And if the mirror breaks he'll be nothing but fragmentary reflections flying through space trying to get himself together again. He can't find a mirror big enough to show him his own ego, Marjorie explains. He resolves to marry her, and beat her with a stick, just in case.

He dreams of a beach endlessly long where he walks forever (see above) towards Marjorie, who is as when young and he first knew her, and naked. And though she's far away and he will never reach her, he knows her body is beaded in seaspray, and her notch of curly black hair will be wet and cold to the touch.

But the beach opens, shifts, divides. The ocean pours down the widening split in the beach. The white cliffs, gulls, blue sky, clouds, shells, harebells, pebbles, seagrass, Marjorie, himself and the whole earth slither in after and he's falling (forever, etc) through everything.

And she's falling away from him. She has shaved her young woman's pubic hair into a black rose, but it makes no difference. Though Thursday week will come for you and I brothers and sisters, for him all the forms in triplicate and the double entry book keeping will never come out straight. It will never again be Friday nor Bognor Regis nor the zoo on a winter afternoon. Goodbye, Harold, just as we've learned your name. We're going off with Marjorie.

Inscription for a book of saints

Let this be a book of misrememberings, mishearings, occasional events, left slippers, secret theatre, a library of last resorts. Let this be my left hand knowing my right scribbling in the dark, my face to the wall I can't see in any case, and goodnight from the Camargue. We are reminded to switch off the set, tidy the kitchen still bloody from a previous nightmare, and put the cat out. Let me be anyone, now, the man known hereabouts as *Parts & Labour*, hired by the gipsies to figure the tarmac and the roofing, impress the farmers with the numbers: that magic. They know him as *College. College will figure it* they say, knowing all the while exactly how they'll settle and what the farmers pay for. We lie to our masters, whoever they are, just as we lie on their behalf, and the truth is always somewhere on the road. Clues as to their thinking, and moments their schemes surface as separate events obliquely reported, if at all, these are to be observed. Whatever Jacob called the angel he wrestled, and wherever that power was from, speaks of another order, if only in the psyche. It is hard work living in a quantum universe, with all the rules running out.

The left slipper

On the 20th March 1980 at 1.45 pm, from a train passing through Clapham Junction on platform 10, beside a station bench a pile of fresh sand and a single red gentleman's left slipper. The slipper looks comfortable, perhaps sheepskin, and worn.

From this event, what possibilities? Are the sand, the bench and the slipper connected other than by proximity, and how many ways might there be a narrative of them? The old man, being taken to the home for old people he doesn't want to go to, deliberately loses it. They think he's daft anyway. Or he throws it in anger, one half of his last Christmas present on Earth rendering the other half useless. Or is one warm foot

142

in fact better than two cold feet? Did they get him on the train, and who are they, and what is their story that they cannot cope with him at home? This is a story you can write yourself. What, for instance, about his being sick as they sat on the bench waiting for the train making cheery remarks like *soon be there Dad*, and humouring him with chocolate digestives?

Richard the Astrologer

I had known him only vaguely years before, in the southern town whose long dream I had lived in, and there been twice bitten. He walked into the Mirabelle where I was drinking with my wife and some friends. In earlier days he had been a figure mooning in the background, a failing student, something of a depressive I had judged or misjudged him. Either way I had always avoided him, and knew nothing more of him than what I have stated. Now he walked in, as if under the same ancient rainy cloud, and recognised me. I nodded, but made no sign of invitation. To my wife I quickly said words I thought to be sufficient of a code for *leave it out. Don't enquire. Don't encourage him.* He would bring with him the names and words of others I'd known, back in the rainy city, and stir the knives in my own dark, whoever he was. I turned back to the circle of conversation.

And yet in five minutes he was in animated conversation with my wife. I felt betrayed, of course, but said nothing on it, and in any case their conversation was short, if vigorous, and soon he was off again. I thought no further of it, then. My surprise came the very next night when, travelling the Northern Line from Camden to Archway, I ran into him again. He told me he'd called my friend at work that day, and was sending her chart. I stared at him. What friend? What chart? *Her birth chart* he said, and then: *I'm an astrologer.* I thought rapidly: *she gave him her name, her work number, her address, her date of birth.* I turned away. I told him I knew nothing of that. I don't know at all about the business of the stars. I told him I had enough trouble understanding the tube map, and getting home.

Home, I was irritable. My wife stared at me, angry in return. *But you introduced him to me* she said. I denied that. *What did I say?* And we compared. What I had said was *Watch out he's from Exeter.* What she

143

had heard was *Richard is an astrologer.* That turned out to be his name, and the profession he professed. Both were true: what I had said; what she had heard.

Between the events, sometimes, a long shadow, a Chinese whisper that turns out to be accurate, like an after voice chasing across the tape, like a footstep always just behind, a true echo.

On a third occasion Richard the Astrologer and I met by chance. Seeing him down the street I set my face against recognition, and walked by him without a flicker on either side, which is the way I want to keep things between him and me.

Russians invented the neutron bomb

It is a meeting of the poets, east and west, for several days, among tall cedars and the green summer of Oxford. We have no common tongue but the rhythms of words, though the East Europeans have some English. When they read their poems it is only the sounds that matter. So here we are. Our governments are not talking to each other, we know so little, we are all from distant countries of which we know nothing much, we may end up on opposite sides of Armageddon. The President of the West believes it may be time to fulfil prophecy, and just before the bombs go off all the born again will float up to heaven in white tunics, and somewhere out of the way of the blast and radiation and the long nuclear winter the Kingdom of God will begin. As for the President of the East, he believes in the certainty of his cause and its victory in which we are the enemy, and he too has no mental apparatus with which to back away from the button. So here we are. So we the poets, we should talk.

And if the angels came, what would they make of it? Observed from the point of view of a hypothetical alien, what would count as typical or normal human behaviour? South Africa? Iran? Central China? Tribal dancing or the rituals of the Freemasons? Bingo? Or the manners of the Surbiton Real Tennis Association? From Alpha Centauri or anywhere there's not a lot of difference between the Ayatollah's beliefs and the convictions of the President of America. Their gods are similar, they don't like women or strong liquor, they believe they're god bidden to make war on those who make war on Earth in league with Satan, they will destroy their enemies who are each other, and each will win.

The Rumanians are having difficulties, holding off, perhaps wary of noisy westerners, perhaps wary of each other. At lunch I approach Gheorghe. I move to sit at his table, and as I do so I accidentally drop my spoon. It clatters on the floor. To cover my clumsiness I make a pointless remark, I say *If Newton hadn't invented gravity I wouldn't have trouble with falling objects.* I pick up my spoon, sit down, shut up.

Gheorghe is angry, and with me. In his little English he tells me so, that I am very wrong, and one day I will regret it. I can't work out what he's talking about, though I try. I have made a silly remark, that's true. Or is it all my life that he objects to? Newton and gravity, I think, are surely no cause for ideological difference. Or is there a Rumanian claim on gravity? And aren't I as ever the innocent, the grinning fool compounding my offence? Gheorghe's anger mounts. I'm no wiser as to its cause. East-West relations between the poets have foundered at the first attempt. My efforts to find the source of anger between mouthfuls of potato salad produce only more confusion, more anger. It's all my fault. Gheorghe continues his denunciation of me: I will regret what I have said. I will regret it bitterly one day. He cannot eat at the same table. He leaves.

I shrug. I eat. I am the victim of language. I will try again, when I've eaten, when temper has cooled perhaps. But temper doesn't cool. Later in the bar I put a drink before Gheorghe, a drink before myself, I sit, I apologise for whatever I have said, I ask if we can start again.

No he says. *No. Not you. Not you and I. It is because you say the Russians invented the neutron bomb. One day you will regret. One day you will know better.* And he leaves. I have failed in my mission. I drink my whisky. Then I drink his. Sorry Gheorghe.

Metro events

I decide to go from Finsbury Park to King's Cross by rail rather than as I usually do by underground. It is a mistake. At the station the tunnels are unfamiliar and mysterious, stairs and stairways and corridors and echoes, all badly labelled as is the way with suburban stations where most of the travellers are commuters who already know the way. I am first warned by the busker in the long tunnel under the tracks, his voice echoing everywhere ahead singing to his guitar *Love is the only way, love is the only way*, over and over. As I pass him, squatting in the long cave among the footsteps, I drop a coin in his upturned hat, and as the coin hits the hat he switches his song, without any break in the beat or the lilt of his voice, and his voice now mocking behind me is singing *You don't need gold, you don't need silver*. At the top of the stairs I can still hear him, singing the same line.

But where's the ticket office? There's only a sign saying *This is not the underground ticket office*, ergo I may buy a train ticket there. I buy a ticket. On the platform there's only a sign saying *Critch & Bollom regret any inconvenience to passengers*, but where is Critch & Bollom? I have the underground map in my head but this is Eastern Region, and I haven't a clue.

A train arrives. The guard gets off, announcing it as an express to King's Cross, so close the train can't have distance enough to be an express. But it will do. But the doors don't open, and if there's a button to press I can't find it, and I can't get on. The train seems unfamiliar. I have a sense of being, suddenly, a clumsy stranger in another country. The train begins moving out. The guard leaps on, and as he passes me I say *What use is this train?* He stops it. *You want to get on?* He seems surprised, and pleased when I say I do. He opens the doors. I get on. The train moves out. I say farewell to Critch & Bollom.

It is a brand new train, clean and fresh smelling. I am the only passenger. A mile or so out of the station it stops in a great field of sidings through which other trains rush north and south, but we do not move. Outside it is dusk, windy north London, distant backyards, paper scraps blown catty corner, high cables singing in the wintry air. We sit there for what seems twenty minutes. I go back to the guard, and ask again what sort of use this train is that's an express. He smiles. He is happy. He tells me this is a new train, a new model of train, the first of its kind, and this is its very first run, and he is the guard. It is an experimental train, he tells me. And I am its first passenger. He's pleased. I'm pleased, I suppose. We talk for another ten minutes, still in the siding, the winter afternoon dying around us, and then we roll at last, and ease into King's Cross the very first of our kind, as if we'd just arrived from some place far away.

The discovery of secret theatre

On another day, another Thursday afternoon, I am alone in a compartment of a Circle Line train stopped at Edgware Road, impatient for my appointment further down the line. At Edgware Road trains die for want of a driver or an engineer or a guard, and I am in one such. There are repeated calls over the loudspeakers for a driver at platform 3. After some five minutes a driver arrives, his jacket over his shoulder, his leather bag across his arm. The engine starts. The doors close. But we're not going anywhere yet. The doors open. The engine dies. The doors close and open again, the engine starts and stops. Everything is tentative. Something is being checked out.

On the last opening and closing three other passengers hurry on, and sit at the far end of the compartment. I observe them. They are a thirtyish man with glasses and a raincoat; an older woman in a blue hat carrying an umbrella; a young woman with long black hair and a black coat, who might be Spanish. The first two sit facing the young woman, but apart. None of these people seem to be together. And then at last the train takes off, towards America and Paddington and Gloucester Road. The young woman lights a cigarette. The older woman leans forward, and politely indicates the no smoking sign. The young woman ignores her. The older woman asks her more pointedly to stop smoking. She doesn't. She crosses her legs, inhales deeply, and stares through the older woman was if she were not present. The man plays no part, takes out a newspaper, and reads it. The train hurtles through the dark, the young woman continues smoking, the older woman moves through all the stages from reasonable request to righteous demand to blazing anger, demanding the other put out her cigarette. She will have her rights. This is a no smoking compartment. She stands up, shouts, waves her arms, stamps her foot, takes off her blue hat and strikes the other hand with it. It's no use. The young woman is unmoved, and continues smoking. When the train stops, she gets up, crushes her cigarette with her high heel, and minces out of the train without a backward glance. The older woman is left, in fury, the target of her anger departed. She sits down, composing herself. The train sets off. The man puts down his newspaper, reaches into his pocket, takes out a cigarette and lights it. What follows is a precise repeat of what went before, until at a further station they both get out. Only I, their audience, remain.

At the Mirabelle

It's a bar, everything as usual, and the moment just as it ought to be: the till clangs, the bottledrop turns, the barman says *what do you think this is?*, there's the nudge music of the video machines, the static on a badly tuned radio behind the bar playing some French station, the street beyond the double glass doors and beyond a van passing by with a sticker that says *read the world*. And why not? Even if it makes little sense I still have to make a living out of it, the world, especially then. I think there are long rhythms we have to stay alive long enough to catch, so long a time falls between beats of it. But now my hand begins to shake a little, when all these years all I was ever trying to do was draw a straight line.

Figuring the present

At Kestor, failing to understand the stoney fields of the iron makers and the purposes of their long raised stones, I discover in the waste among the little stars of the moss a single blue child's sock.

Cogito at the British Museum
(for ZH)

His train climbs out of the earth towards the embankment, and sails over the river. He is glimpsing the old waterway of the wooded settlement, the triremes riding at anchor in the tide pull. Suddenly there are too many national symbols at once: the mother of parliaments fluffed out in scaffolding like a Chinese pagoda, and her clock all the country turns to, and the old voice of John Snagge announcing the D-Day landings. He walks out into daylight and travels the city among the photographs of victory, the flags and statues, he reads beneath Scott's memorial *only these rough notes and our dead bodies must tell the tale*, he thinks of everyone as a torn piece of paper in the wind bearing just a bit of message. It is a shame about the governments, the sleeve tuggers, the time servers, the party hacks. *Fox with fox* he says. *Party dog with party dog.* He takes a taxi, and thinks of Blake talking with Isaiah, and

148

feels pleasantly invisible among the tourists and the tight security.

At the museum they study his passport and his letter of introduction. They agree he is a professor of credibility, in permanent exile in the interior of his life, a scholar who has studied alchemy astronomy calligraphy invisibility philately and whisky, reading only page 23 of each volume. Satisfied he carries no bombs in his briefcase, no knives, no automatic pistols, they take his photograph, issue him an i.d., and admit him. He is looking for a particular book, and hasn't found it in Berlin or Paris. He cannot find it here either. He examines catalogues, distracted by the titles and authors of books he's not travelled so far to look at, but can't find the one he wants. It isn't listed. Perhaps it was never published. Perhaps he only imagined it. It is a book no one ever wrote.

He enquires. Directed to another section he enquires again, consults a further index, is passed to another desk, knocks at another office, is referred to another department. It is all familiar, the long footsteps, the heavy curtains in the corridor, the knock of varnished wood, the walls of books towering over him, the light's reflections in the glass cases. And always the book he cannot find, and the polite officials who cannot find the book. And now there's only one place left to look. They send him there. It's called the Library of Last Resorts. He waits there, numbering off his ordinary tragedies, his many dress rehearsals for the undertaker. He lists the days of his life, his disappearing acts, his silences, his fortunate ability to see himself in the third person. *To lose a country, that is careless* he whispers to himself. *But now to lose the book of it.*

The weaving irregularities
and shade variations are
characteristic of tne fabric
and in no way to be taken
as defects

Attractively fizzy...Smith's prevailing tone might be dubbed 'bossy hedonism'. He has all the chip-on-the-shoulder characteristics of the anti-Establishment poet, but he has other less common features — humour, a sense of the ridiculous, delicacy of association and romantic fervour.
● **THE OBSERVER/Peter Porter**

A splendidly spirited performance, a volume full of humour, anger, affection and indignation. Smith's wild energy pulsates through the poems... His imaginatively produced book shows him in fine form as one of the most muscular of modern English poets.
● **THE SCOTSMAN/Alan Bold**

He is a populist without being shallow and he writes with what an American would call 'balls' and we would term 'guts'.
● **BRITISH BOOK NEWS/Martin Booth**

TERRA **is Ken Smith's latest book of poems. It is a Poetry Book Society Recommendation, and was also shortlisted for the Whitbread Prize. The book includes his new LONDON POEMS, the cryptic IGNORE PREVIOUS TELEGRAM, and HAWKWOOD, the secret journal of a 14th century mercenary.**

He plants brass knuckles and torn linen verse onto your pages, holds up his heart, still pulsing and palpitating, in front of your face. And boyoboy, does he ever look the part! This is an impressive impression, handsomely laid out and tersely terse with a cover of boiling lava. Very Nice.
● **BLITZ**

I've joined the Rupert Bear School of Poetry and I'll not say anything controversial.
● **THE BOTANIC GARDEN OATH**

TERRA

KEN SMITH

The Poet Reclining

Selected Poems 1962-1980

● VISCERAL VERSE

Ken Smith is a poet of formidable range and strength who has absorbed the life and landscape of America as well as that of Europe and of his own Yorkshire background. He cultivates a voice which is personal, yet much more than personal: the result of having opened up hidden layers of common fear, suffering and desire.
● **CHICAGO SUN-TIMES/Ralph J Mills**

His images read as if they were wrenched from the innards of his own experience and his verse manages to communicate on a basic, visceral level.
● **THE SCOTSMAN/Alan Bold**

THE POET RECLINING is Ken Smith's Selected Poems. It includes his major long poem Fox Running.

● HEAVY BREATHER

Ken Smith is so unswervingly serious a poet, such a heavy breather down the line to intensity.
● **THE OBSERVER/Peter Porter**

Recently, Smith has written increasingly important verse in which, in a less critical but more trenchant manner, he threatens even Larkin as a leading social poet. His sequence **Fox Running** is as important as Hughes's **Crow** poems as an innovative group.
● **TRIBUNE/Martin Booth**

● **Ken Smith**: 'common fear, suffering and desire'

KEN SMITH

should be etched on every poet's heart, or failing that, the study wall: 'don't lie to those people within you, they'll find out'.
● **PN REVIEW/Ian McMillan**

● **S H A T T E R I N G   L I N E S**

This volume pretends to be the surviving fragments of a library assembled by President Perdu, an elitist dictator whose fall from power was attended by the mysterious firing of his collection. The very structure of the book is teasing, for our image of the despot relies on snippets and clues to his character from the salvaged remains of his taste, and some of his own compositions.
● **THE LITERARY REVIEW/David Profumo**

Witty pieces combine with gleaming fragmented poems like 'From Belmont, A Ghetto Song', with its shattering lines: 'On the wall a child's scrawl/ I hate me', and 'They never complain/ to whom nothing is promised', and, from 'Nicholson's advice', lines which

Lives ago, years past generations
perhaps nowhere I dreamed it:
the foggy ploughland of wind
and hoofprints, my father
off in the mist topping beets.

Where I was eight, I knew nothing,
the world a cold winter light
on half a dozen fields, then
all the winking blether of stars.

Before like a fool I began
explaining the key in it lost locked box
adding words to the words to the sum
that never works out.
                         Where I was
distracted again by the lapwing,
the damp morning air of my father's
gregarious plainchant cursing
all that his masters deserved
and had paid for.
                         Sure I was
then for the world's mere being
in the white rime on weeds
among the wet hawthorn berries
at the field's edge darkened by frost,
and none of these damned words to say it.

I began trailing out there in voices,
friends, women, my children,
my father's tetherless anger, some
like him who are dead who are
part of the rain now.

● **B E I N G   T H E   T H I R D
S O N G   O F   U R I A S**
From THE POET RECLINING

BURNED BOOKS

THE POETRY IS NOT ENGLISH. It has escaped from the bounds of insularity and is not only universal in content but also wide in appeal . . .

His poetry is primal and basic . . . <u>Fox Running</u> uses a period of breakdown to construct a series of poems about a poet lost in the metropolis of slums and poverty, seeking himself and a way out of his inner and outer states of destitution. This may sound selfish and narrow, but Smith is never that. **He writes to people rather than for them** and it is upon this that he must base a good deal of his success. It might also account for his having been outside in the poetic wilderness for many years, unheeded by editors and many of his peers alike. **He is frankly too good** and must pose a threat to others.

● From **BRITISH POETRY 1964-1984: DRIVING THROUGH THE BARRICADES** by **Martin Booth** (Routledge, 1985)

● **Ken Smith**: 'He is frankly too good'

●**Ken Smith** was born in 1938 in East Rudston, Yorkshire, the son of an itinerant farm labourer. He has worked in Britain and America as a teacher, freelance writer, barman, magazine editor, potato picker and BBC reader, and has held writing fellowships at Leeds University, Kingston Polytechnic, and Clark University and Holy Cross, Worcester, Massachusetts. While living in America he served a term as poet in the Toledo House of Correction. He is now writer-in-residence at Wormwood Scrubs prison. His first book **The Pity** was published by Jonathan Cape in 1967, and his second **Work, distances/poems** by Swallow Press, Chicago, in 1972. Poems from these two collections and from numerous other books and pamphlets published between 1964 and 1980 (including **Fox Running**) were brought together in his Bloodaxe Selected **The Poet Reclining** (1982). Also available from Bloodaxe are his **Abel Baker Charlie Delta Epic Sonnets** (1982) and **Burned Books** (1981). His latest book of poems is **Terra** (1985), a Poetry Book Society Recommendation.

KEN SMITH